End-Time
Living

End-Time Living

Living

Essential Truths for Troubled Times

Mark A. Finley

Pacific Press® Publishing Association
Nampa, Idaho
Oshawa, Ontario, Canada
www.pacificpress.com

Cover design by Gerald Lee Monks
Cover photo by iStockPhoto.com

Unless otherwise indicated, Scripture quotations are from
the New King James Version.

ISBN 13: 978-0-8163-2174-2
ISBN 10: 0-8163-2174-4

Additional copies of this book are available by calling
toll-free 1-800-765-6955 or by visiting
<http://www.adventistbookcenter.com>.

06 07 08 09 10 • 5 4 3 2 1

Contents

Eden and the End Time

Tina's father had been a dockworker for most of her life. Once, this man had changed her diapers and taught her to ride a bike. But cancer reduced him to a frail, disoriented fragment of himself, and then it killed him.

Tina thought she could just go on with life after the funeral. But nothing was quite the same. Her father's absence haunted her. The scent of Old Spice aftershave or the sound of one of his favorite songs would move her to tears. Tina says, "I know I'm an adult and I'm supposed to be strong, but on some days I feel like I'm four years old and all I want is my dad."

Have you ever felt that way? We experience a haunting emptiness when we're separated from those we love. We know a sense of loneliness that none but those closest to us can fill.

Death was never part of God's original plan. It wasn't part of His design for the human race. It wasn't in His blueprint for a happy, abundant life. According to Genesis, when God created this world, He "saw everything that He had made, and indeed it was very good" (Genesis 1:31). Then an intruder interrupted God's plan. An evil one appeared in the Garden and deceived our first parents, and like storm clouds suddenly appearing on the horizon on a warm summer day, sickness, suffering, sorrow, and death descended upon the human family.

Out of the tragedy of humankind's fall into sin recorded in Genesis 3, four eternal lessons for end-time living unfold. Echoes from Eden speak to our hearts in the twenty-first century. Understanding the Bible's beginning in Genesis prepares us to understand its ending in Revelation. The devil's deceptions in earth's last days will be the same as those he used during the early days of earth's history. Times have changed, but his strategy has not.

Our choices have eternal consequences

In Eden, the evil one's temptation began with these fateful words: " 'Has God indeed said, "You shall not eat of every tree of the garden"?' " (Genesis 3:1). The devil stirred up the dust storm of doubt. His intent was to lead Eve to doubt God. He insinuated that God was unfair. He suggested that God didn't have Eve's best interest at heart and that He couldn't be trusted. The devil's subtle temptation focused on the issue of choice. He convinced Eve that she would be much happier if she followed her own independent judgment; that she was sufficiently intelligent to choose what she believed would make her happy, so why should she obey God? Here is the devil's fundamental lie: Happiness comes from a life lived independently from God. God's commands are restrictive and arbitrary. They limit life's greatest joys.

Satan has not changed his methods very much at all. Many people depend on their own minds to provide their only criteria for right and wrong. They don't believe there are any absolutes. They think that nothing in and of itself is always right or wrong. People in the twenty-first century commonly believe that every person must establish what is "right" for himself or herself.

According to a recent survey by the Barna Research Group, Gen-Xers boycott the idea of absolute truth. In fact, the staggering reality is that "seventy-five percent of adults and teens reject the concept of absolute moral truth." In other words, the matter of what constitutes right and wrong is as subjective as your own thoughts and feelings.

Joseph Fletcher popularized this view forty years ago in his book *Situation Ethics*. He said that adultery, lying, stealing, or breaking any of the other of the Ten Commandments is not necessarily always wrong. If the situation is right, the act may be right. And more than one half of all teenagers today say that lying is sometimes necessary—not merely convenient, common, understandable, or acceptable but *necessary!*

What is essentially wrong with the idea that all of us must determine right and wrong for ourselves? It is precisely this: It places human beings above God.

The God who made us knows best how we ought to live. His commands are eternal guarantees of inner happiness. Our faulty judgment does not determine right. God's Word does. Our changing feelings are not the basis for morality. God's unchanging commands are.

Our choices have eternal consequences. Eve's choice certainly did. Genesis records that choice this way. "So when the woman saw that the tree was good for food, that it was pleasant to the eyes, and a tree desirable to make one wise, she took of its fruit and ate" (Genesis 3:6). It is clear: The choice to eat was Eve's. Adam joined his beautiful wife in that choice. No one forced them to choose to disobey God. No one coerced them. No one chose for them. They chose to believe the words of Satan and to disbelieve the words of God.

Adam and Eve were deceived. Deception is substituting a lie in place of the truth. And the results of their choice were disastrous. While the eternal principles of truth in God's Word are life-giving, the consequences of disobedience are devastating. The landscape of life is littered with the corpses disobedience has produced. Hollow men and women live battered, bruised, broken, bloodied lives. Many are empty shells longing for meaning, purpose, and direction. They have followed their own inclinations through the darkened doorway of disaster.

When God placed our first parents in their garden home, He gave them the power of choice. They were not predestined to fall—victims of some cosmic plot or puppets manipulated by divine strings. The essence of the image of God is the ability to make moral choices. Our freedom of choice is the heart of what it means to be human. And God so values our freedom of choice that in order to preserve our ability to choose He even allows us to make wrong choices.

Cain's uncontrolled anger led him to murder his brother, and he spent the rest of his life running. David's uncontrolled lust led him to commit adultery with Bathsheba, and although he experienced forgiveness, his actions devastated his family relations. Judas's uncontrolled desire for money led him to sell his Lord cheap, and despite the potential his many talents held, his life ended much too soon.

But while poor choices lead to heartbreaking results, good choices lead to positive results. The history of Egypt was changed because Joseph resisted the improper advances of Potiphar's wife. He chose the moral high road, and God honored him with one of the highest positions in the nation.

The history of Babylon was changed because Daniel "purposed in his heart" to serve God. Daniel controlled his desires, and God led him to guide two world empires—Babylon and Media-Persia.

The history of the Roman Empire was changed because Paul refused to bow down to Roman idols. Christ, not Caesar, was the center of Paul's life, and the conquests of the Cross were far greater than the exploits of Rome.

Similarly, our choices make an incredible difference in our lives—and it is never too late to begin to make positive choices. The sooner we do, the sooner good things will begin to happen.

I met Pat and Joe in the early 1980s. They were living in a suburb of Chicago. The passionate pursuit of pleasure consumed them—they loved to party, and alcohol was at the center of their lives. They could hardly believe that people could be happy without a drink.

These two people were going steadily downhill. They were crowded into a small apartment. Their finances were tight. And they were finding it increasingly difficult to function; they seemed to be locked into negative thought patterns and destructive behaviors.

Together, Pat, Joe, and I opened God's Word. Christ's love charmed them. His willingness to forgive touched them at the core of their being. His power to heal the sick, calm the storm, multiply the bread, and deliver demoniacs overwhelmed them. They longed for His deliverance and yearned for His power.

One of the most memorable nights of my life was the night we claimed our Lord's promise in Philippians 4:13, "I can do all things through Christ who strengthens me." That night we partied together. I invited them to bring all of their alcohol and place it on the dining-room table. As I recall, there were at least two six packs of beer, three bottles of wine, and a couple bottles of Scotch.

We sang hymns. We prayed. We claimed Bible promises. Then we popped corks, opened cans, and unscrewed caps. And we rejoiced in the power of God to deliver us from evil as we poured the beer, wine, and Scotch down the toilet. Pat and Joe felt liberated. They were no longer controlled by alcohol.

We continued our weekly visits, and they gradually became strong Christians. Positive choices led to positive results, and a new peace flooded into their lives. Eventually, their economic situation changed. They moved out of their small apartment, started their own motel business, and prospered physically, mentally, spiritually, and economically.

God calls those of us living during the end time to moral responsibility for our choices. Revelation, the last book of the Bible, announces that the hour of God's judgment has come (see Revelation 14:7). Judgment implies moral accountability. We are responsible for our actions, and excuses won't do. Genesis, the book of beginnings, and Revelation, the book of endings, shout at us in trumpet tones "choices bring eternal consequences."

Substitutes don't work

These Bible books also reveal that substitutes don't work. Let's turn our minds back to Eden again. Genesis 3:7, 8 reveals another eternal truth: When we turn from God's way, we seek substitutes to ease the pain in our hearts. This passage says that Adam and Eve "sewed fig leaves together and made themselves coverings. . . . And Adam and his wife hid themselves from the presence of the LORD God."

Adam and Eve covered themselves physically with the fig leaves, but spiritually they were naked. Sin brings a nakedness of soul—our first parents lost the security, peace, joy, health, and stability God gave them when He created them. Instead, they were filled with despair, depression, despondency, degradation, and death.

In 1923, a group of the world's wealthiest men met in Chicago's Edgewater Beach Hotel on the shores of Lake Michigan to discuss the economic future of America. The group included:

- The president of the largest independent steel company
- The president of the largest utility company
- The president of the largest gas company
- The president of the New York Stock Exchange
- A member of the U. S. president's cabinet
- The wealthiest investor on Wall Street
- The head of the world's largest monopoly
- The president of the Bank of International Settlements

If success means position, power, influence, money, and reputation, this certainly was a gathering of the world's most successful men. But were these men really successful? Does substituting position, power, and financial success in place of Jesus Christ really bring happiness? Does abandoning the eternal principles of God's Word bring lasting peace and inner meaning? What was the result of substituting the "fig leaf" garments of human success for the light of God's glorious presence?

- The president of the largest independent steel company, Charles M. Schwab, had to live on borrowed money the last five years of his life, and he died bankrupt.
- The president of the largest utility company, Samuel Insull, died a fugitive from justice, penniless in a foreign land.
- The president of the largest gas company, Howard Hopson, went insane.
- The president of the New York Stock Exchange, Richard Whitney, was judged guilty of fraud and spent the rest of his life in Sing Sing Penitentiary.
- Albert Fall, the member of the president's cabinet, was sentenced to prison and eventually pardoned to die at home.
- The wealthiest investor on Wall Street, Jesse Livermore, died a suicide.
- The head of the greatest monopoly, Ivan Kruger, died a suicide.
- The president of the Bank of International Settlements, Leon Fraser, died a suicide.

Each of these men achieved status, fame, and fortune but they were spiritually naked. Their souls were barren. Their hearts were restless. Their lives were empty. Position, power, fame, and fortune do not satisfy. These "fig leaf" garments woven together by human hands leave us naked. They don't produce joy, happiness, security, or freedom from guilt.

But God had a plan for our first parents, and He has a plan for us too. Genesis 3:21 states it clearly:

"For Adam and his wife the LORD God made tunics of skin, and clothed them" (Genesis 3:21).

God did what Adam and Eve could not do. He met their needs. He took away the "fig leaves" of their own making, and wrapped them with clothing that He supplied. He clothed them with

- His love
- His grace
- His goodness
- His mercy
- His forgiveness
- His security
- His promise of a new future

God clothed Adam and Eve with hope in the promise of a dying Savior and a coming Messiah. He met the needs of their heart. He met the longing of their soul. He met the cry of their spirit. No substitute will do. There is only One who can meet our innermost needs. The old hymn states it well.

There's not a friend like the lowly Jesus,
No, not one! No, not one!
None else could heal all our soul's diseases,
No, not one! No, not one!
There's not an hour that He is not near us,
No, not one! No, not one!

There is no substitute for the peace Christ can bring. There is no substitute for the forgiveness the

Savior offers. There are many counterfeits, but no substitute for His life-changing power. Positive living begins when we take responsibility for our actions and seek God's strength to change our lives.

Change comes through taking responsibility

Did you notice how our first parents failed initially to take any responsibility for their actions? Adam blamed Eve, and Eve blamed the serpent. But God swept away their false disguise. He laid bare their excuses. He said, "Because you ate of the fruit . . ." (see Genesis 3:17). God was saying to Adam, "Stop making excuses."

We'll never experience positive change as long as we attempt to justify our behavior. As long as we are locked in the downward spiral of victimization, we'll never break out of bondage. People who are victims of circumstances rather than change agents through their own choices will never be really free.

Did you ever hear the baloney sandwich story? Every day two construction workers, Steve and Rick, ate lunch together. Day in and day out, Steve ate the same thing—a baloney sandwich.

One day Steve looked at Rick and said, "I hate baloney sandwiches!"

Rick responded, "Why don't you tell your wife? I'm sure she'd pack something else for you."

"Oh," Steve said, "I pack the baloney myself."

Most of the baloney in our lives is there because we packed it ourselves. Often we excuse our behavior with comments like these:

- "I know my temper is kind of out of control, but you should meet my father. I guess I'm cut from the same cloth."
- "I really should control my appetite better, but everyone in my family is overweight."
- "I realize my drinking is out of hand, but I'm under a lot of stress."
- "I know I should attend church more often, but I'm just too tired on the weekend."
- "I really would like to pray and study the Bible more, but I'm just too busy."

Change comes when we take personal responsibility for our attitude and behavior. When we don't take ownership of our current actions and attitudes, we'll experience no change.

A young couple who were having a real challenge with debt discovered a solution—"plastic surgery." They took responsibility. They got out a pair of scissors and cut up their credit cards. They kept only one and determined to limit the amount they put on it each month.

A middle-aged woman who discovered that she was being controlled by a negative, critical spirit discovered a solution. She took responsibility and got a "heart transplant." Twice each morning she knelt before the Lord to thank Him for His goodness, to think consciously of the positive things in her life, and to look for traits in others to praise rather than to criticize.

A young executive who was consumed by the desire to make money took responsibility. Throughout the day, he asked God to supply him with "corrective lenses" so he could take the long view and discover what really mattered.

Love takes the initiative

So, Eden's eternal lessons reveal that each choice has eternal consequences, substitutes don't work, and change comes by taking responsibility. It also reveals that love takes the initiative.

When our first parents fell in Eden, God took the initiative. His voice of love echoed through the Garden as He graciously called out to His lost children (see Genesis 3:9). And speaking in symbols, He declared that eventually the Savior would bruise the devil's head, but in the effort, the devil would bruise His heel (Genesis 3:15).

Jesus was willing to be bruised so we could be healed. He left the glories of heaven and came to this sin-cursed earth so that we could leave this sin-cursed earth and ascend to the glories of heaven. He was innocent but took upon Himself our guilt so that we who are guilty can have His innocence. He was righteous but took upon Himself our unrighteousness so that we who are unrighteous could have His righteousness. He, the King of kings, became servant of all so that we who are in bondage to the slavery of sin could become sons and daughters of the King of the universe. Jesus, the One who is love, came on a mission of love to minister in love to redeem a people in desperate need of love.

Now, the Voice heard in Eden speaks to a generation living in the end time. Jesus speaks of vital, everyday choices that have eternal consequences. He speaks of our foolish attempts to cover our spiritual nakedness with substitutes that didn't work then and won't work now. He issues a clarion call to take responsibility—to become accountable for our actions. He speaks of a love that longs to fill our hearts with assurance, security, forgiveness, and power.

Love for His lost children overflows from Jesus' heart. He longs for us to live abundant, happy lives. After all, that's what He created us for, what He intended us to know—until Satan spoiled His plan. End-time living is not gritting our teeth and clenching our fists in agony until He returns. It is rejoicing in His love, resting in His grace, and receiving His abundance.

Living successfully at the end time means choosing God's way, not our own. If you haven't done it already, why not do it today?

Prophecy's Big Picture

The year was 1991. Communism had crumbled. The Berlin Wall had come down. Freedom was in the air in Eastern Europe. The Soviet Union opened to the gospel, and night after night, I preached to packed audiences in the Plehanof University auditorium in Moscow.

One evening, a frail, middle-aged woman approached me and said, "Pastor, I too am a Christian. Please come visit me at my home. I would gladly feed you supper."

My wife and I accepted her kind invitation, and when we arrived at her very modest apartment, she enthusiastically welcomed us with open arms. We were somewhat embarrassed with all the attention she gave us. It was obvious that she had prepared for two or three days to feed us. At that time, the average monthly salary in Moscow was twenty-eight dollars. As I looked at the dinner table laden with fresh fruits and set for a four-course meal, I knew this woman had spent more than her entire month's salary on the food. My discomfort level grew as this humble family in a little three-room apartment treated us as royalty. They seemed to want to know everything about America—where we lived, what our house was like, what we liked to eat, and scores of other details about our personal lives.

In an attempt to get the attention off us, I asked, "What was the most difficult situation you ever faced as a Christian under the communist regime?"

The woman's lips began to quiver, her body trembled, her hands shook, and she began to sob. My translator gripped my hand and said, "Pastor Mark, don't lead this poor woman down this path. The memories are too painful. She may have an anxiety attack."

But it was too late. The secrets she had kept hidden in her heart for decades tumbled out. She responded, "Pastor, the most difficult experience I ever had under communism was when the KGB [Russian secret police] learned that I was teaching my two daughters about Jesus. An informant living in an apartment above me tipped them off. The police discovered I conducted worship with my children each day. They found out we sang Christian hymns and studied the Bible together. One evening, they burst into my home and seized my nine-year-old daughter. I still remember her cries, 'Mama, Mama, please help me!' They carried her out the door, and I could do nothing. I was powerless to help her."

"Pastor," the woman continued, "that was twenty-eight years ago, and I haven't seen her since."

As I looked into those tear-stained eyes, I thought of the pain that pierced her heart like a sword. Then her voice broke, and she said, "Pastor, I know I will see my daughter again when Jesus comes. We will be reunited. No one will be able to separate us then. We will be together with Jesus forever."

This woman's hope is prophecy's big picture. We can become so caught up in the details of prophecy that we miss the big picture. Jesus describes the big picture this way: " 'Let not your heart be troubled; you believe in God, believe also in Me. In My Father's house are many mansions; if it were not so, I would have told you. I go to prepare a place for you. And if I go and prepare a place for you, I will come again and receive you to Myself; that where I am, there you may be also' " (John 14:1–3).

The second coming of Christ provides hope for troubled hearts. Soon Jesus will come. Soon the heartache and sorrows of life will be over. There may be many things about the future we wish we knew. There may be many things about prophecy we wish we could explain. But there's something more important than the details of prophecy. Knowing the end of prophecy—the conclusion toward which it points—is more important than understanding all the details. The big picture of prophecy is more important than the pieces in the puzzle.

There are millions of people who want to understand every aspect of prophecy but who miss its climax.

They have their eyes fixed on what the devil is doing, not on what Christ will do. But all prophecies point to Jesus. He is the climax of all prophecy. History is not an endless cycle of events. All of history is moving toward one colossal event, the second coming of our Lord.

Two books of the Bible—Daniel in the Old Testament and Revelation in the New—focus particularly on the climax of history. The ancient Bible prophets bring courage to our generation. Their focus is not on disaster but on deliverance. Their emphasis is not on a coming catastrophe; it is upon a coming Christ. They speak not of a tragic ending but of a glorious beginning. They who wrote Daniel and Revelation present a new world, a better world. They help us reach out and touch the kingdom of God. They give us glimpses of eternity. They help us see the big picture. Let's take a brief journey together through Daniel and Revelation. Let's catch the inspiration of these hope-filled books.

A future-revealing dream

In 605 B.C., King Nebuchadnezzar of Babylon attacked and overthrew Jerusalem. Nebuchadnezzar took a significant number of Hebrew youth captive. One of his captives was Daniel. John, the author of Revelation, was a captive in a foreign land too. The last of the living disciples, he was exiled by the Romans to the island of Patmos, off the coast of Asia Minor.

Both Daniel and John longed for deliverance. They anticipated the day when sin and suffering would be no more—a day when conflict and chaos would be gone. They looked forward to a bright tomorrow when disease, disaster, devastation, destruction, and death would fade away in the glory of a new world. God honored these Bible stalwarts' faithfulness by showing them prophecy's big picture. He opened their eyes to eternity.

The second chapter of the book of Daniel opens with the dream of the Babylonian king Nebuchadnezzar. "Now in the second year of Nebuchadnezzar's reign, Nebuchadnezzar had dreams; and his spirit was so troubled that his sleep left him" (Daniel 2:1).

Nebuchadnezzar knew his dream had unusual significance, but he couldn't remember its contents. He called the wisest men of his realm together for an explanation, but they could neither tell the king his forgotten dream nor explain its significance. Infuriated, the king threatened them with death. At this crisis moment, Daniel stepped forward. He graciously requested time to pray about the unsolved mystery. And God intervened. He revealed heaven's mystery.

The content of the dream is obvious from Daniel's prayer of thanksgiving. It reveals a God who " 'changes the times and the seasons; He removes kings and raises up kings. . . . He reveals deep and secret things' " (verses 21, 22). Since " 'wisdom and might' " (verse 20) are God's, He not only knows the future; He is its architect.

Bible prophets don't speculate about the future. They don't guess about what might be coming. In the Scriptures, they reveal to us what God has revealed to them. Daniel clearly explained what King Nebuchad-nezzar dreamed. " 'You, O king, were watching; and behold, a great image!' " (verse 31). The prophet then described this awesome figure. The huge metallic image had a head of gold, breast and arms of silver, thighs of brass, legs of iron, and feet of iron and clay (see verses 31–33). In the climax of the king's dream, a massive stone destroys the image and then becomes a mountain that fills the whole earth.

Think of how amazed the ancient king must have been when the prophet Daniel described the minute details of his dream! The king's next question must have been, "Daniel, what does all of this mean?" Daniel's explanation of the dream's meaning is just as precise as his description of the dream's content. He begins the explanation with these words: " 'You are this head of gold. But after you shall arise another kingdom inferior to yours; then another, a third kingdom of bronze, which shall rule over all the earth. And the fourth kingdom shall be as strong as iron' " (verses 38–40).

According to God's interpretation through the prophet Daniel, the dream depicts the rise and fall of nations. Each metal represents an empire. Daniel identifies Nebuchadnezzar's kingdom of Babylon with the words "You are this head of gold." The Babylonian Empire ruled the Middle East from 605 B.C. to 539 B.C.

Gold is a fitting symbol of Babylon. That nation's chief god, Bel-Marduk, was symbolized in a statue of pure gold. This golden image of Bel-Marduk sat in a golden-domed temple on a golden throne beneath a golden candlestick before a golden table. Babylon's lifestyle of luxurious living led Jeremiah the prophet to call Babylon "a golden cup in the Lord's hand" (Jeremiah 51:7).

This incredible prophecy in Daniel 2 reveals that Babylon would not rule forever. "Another kingdom," symbolized by the breast and arms of silver, would arise. During a night of drunken debauchery, a mysterious hand wrote these words on Babylon's palace wall: " 'God has numbered your kingdom, and finished it; . . . You have been weighed in the balances, and found wanting; . . . Your kingdom has been divided, and given to the Medes and Persians' " (Daniel 5:26–28).

There is no guesswork or speculation here. The kingdom that followed Babylon was Media-Persia. Both the Bible and history verify this fact. The famed Cyrus cylinder housed in the British Museum records Cyrus the Persian's attack on Babylon. The Medes and Persians ruled from 539 B.C. to 381 B.C.

A third empire, one symbolized by the brass section of the image, would overcome the "breast and arms of silver." What nation successfully conquered Media-Persia? The Greeks defeated this empire in 331 B.C. The brilliant general Alexander the Great led the Greek armies to victory. Daniel 8 describes the Greeks by name as vanquishing Media-Persia. Both Scripture and history agree. The Greeks ruled from 331 B.C. to 168 B.C., when the iron monarchy of Rome defeated them.

Jesus was born during the rule of the Caesars. At the end of His life, a Roman governor tried Him, and

Roman soldiers crucified Him. The Romans ruled from 168 B.C. to approximately A.D. 351.

Nebuchadnezzar's dream pictured four metals—gold, silver, brass, and iron—that represented four dominant kingdoms—Babylon, Media-Persia, Greece, and Rome. Did another more powerful political power conquer the fourth empire? Did a fifth world-ruling empire overthrow Rome? Certainly not. Germanic tribes from the north overcame Rome. Listen to these remarkable words from the prophecy: " 'Whereas you saw the feet and toes, partly of potter's clay and partly of iron, the kingdom shall be divided' " (Daniel 2:41). History has followed prophecy as a builder follows an architect's blueprint. The Roman Empire was divided and remains divided even now.

The prophecy says, " 'They will not adhere to one another, just as iron does not mix with clay' " (verse 43). Each passing century marks the continuing fulfillment of this ancient prophecy. Would-be world rulers have tried to revive the Roman Empire. Charlemagne, Charles V, Napoleon, Kaiser Wilhelm, Hitler, Mussolini, and Stalin all attempted to unite Europe through either intermarriage or political conquest. But the independent nations of Europe speak eloquently of a God who is in control, a God who guides the destiny of the nations.

Next on heaven's timetable

The prophecy comes to an incredible climax in Daniel 2:44: " 'In the days of these kings the God of heaven will set up a kingdom which shall never be destroyed; and the kingdom shall not be left to other people; it shall break in pieces and consume all these kingdoms, and it shall stand forever.' " According to this remarkable prophecy, the next event on heaven's timetable is the coming of Jesus Christ. The Rock of Ages—that Rock cut out without hands (see verse 34)—will set up His eternal, everlasting kingdom.

The kingdoms of this earth are temporary. God's kingdom will last forever. The reign of earthly kings is short-lived. Jesus' reign is eternal. The prophecies of both Daniel and Revelation picture one glorious, climactic event on the horizon—the return of the Lord Jesus Christ.

Each successive end-time prophecy in the book of Daniel repeats the central theme of the earlier ones and enlarges upon them. Repetition and enlargement are God's way of helping us understand prophecy's genuine meaning. In Daniel 2, God uses four metals to symbolize four mighty kingdoms. In Daniel 7, God uses four beasts to symbolize the same four nations. And the beasts that God chooses to represent these nations are fitting descriptions of each of them. Once again, we don't have to guess at the meaning of this prophetic symbolism. The same God who reveals prophecy explains prophecy.

According to Daniel 7:17, " ' "Those great beasts, which are four, are four kings [or kingdoms; see verse 23] which arise out of the earth." ' " In the magnificent vision that God gave Daniel, He pictured these beasts rising up out of a fiercely stormy sea, in the midst of mighty winds. In Bible prophecy, the sea or water represents people (see Revelation 17:15), and wind represents destruction, devastation, and disaster (see Jeremiah 49:36, 37). So Daniel's prophecy predicts nations arising amidst the conflict of war.

The first beast, the lion with eagle's wings (see Daniel 7:4), is an accurate representation of the nation of Babylon. Archeologists have discovered this "lion with eagle's wings" symbol on the walls of the city of Babylon and on coins excavated from the ruins of that city.

The Medes and Persians were aptly described by the ruthlessness of a bear with three ribs in its mouth (see verse 5). It is interesting to note that to dominate the Middle East, the Medes and Persians had to conquer three nations—Babylon, Lydia, and Egypt. The prophecy represents these defeated nations by the three ribs.

The swiftness of Alexander the Great's conquests are graphically revealed in the symbolism of a leopard with wings (see verse 6). This third beast, the leopard, has four heads. Why? When Alexander died, his four generals—Cassandra, Lysimachus, Ptolemy, and Seleucus—took over his empire.

The fourth beast is pictured as incredibly fierce and amazingly powerful, with huge iron teeth (see verse 7). And this "dreadful" beast has ten horns (see verse 7). The beast represents the Roman Empire, and the horns symbolize nations that took its place.

It is at this point in the prophecy that God introduces a completely new element. Until now, political powers have attempted to usurp God's rightful position as the One who truly reigns over this earth. In Daniel 7:8, a little-horn power—a power that begins small but is catapulted into world dominance—grows quietly out of Rome. According to the prophecy, this power has " 'eyes like the eyes of a man' " (verse 8). Eyes in the Bible represent wisdom or understanding (see Ephesians 1:18). The authority of this power is human, not divine. It is based on human wisdom, not God's Word. It would ultimately "cast truth down to the ground" (Daniel 8:12).

This little-horn power growing out of Rome " ' "shall speak pompous words against the Most High, shall persecute the saints of the Most High, and shall intend to change times and law" ' " (Daniel 7:25). This little-horn power would be "different" from all other powers mentioned in this chapter (see verse 23). The prophecy indicates that this power is religious as well as political (see verses 24, 25). A counterfeit political-religious system arises out of Rome that attempts to usurp God's authority by changing His law. God's answer to the challenge of the little horn is His final judgment (see verses 21, 22). The little horn claims to represent true religion, but it doesn't. The judgment sweeps away all pretense. It exposes all falsity. It reveals all hypocrisy.

The prophecy's triumphant end

All the prophecies of Daniel end in the same place—the establishment of God's eternal kingdom. Catch the triumphant tone of the final verses of this amazing prophecy: " ' "But the court shall be seated, and they shall take away his dominion, to consume and destroy it forever. Then the kingdom and dominion, and the greatness of the kingdoms under the whole heaven, shall be given to the people, the saints of the Most High. His kingdom is an everlasting kingdom, and all dominions shall serve and obey Him" ' " (verses 26, 27). Though earth's kingdoms crumble, God's kingdom lasts forever.

The prophecies of Daniel all have one central theme. They have a single, sharp focus—the triumph of God's eternal kingdom in the return of our Lord. This is true of all four great lines of prophecy in the book of Daniel—chapters 2, 7, 8, and 11.

The prophecies of Daniel and Revelation don't picture a secret rapture. When Jesus came the first time, He came quietly as a babe in Bethlehem's manger. Only a few recognized Him. The majority of the world had no idea that the Messiah was born.

When He comes again in power and glory and splendor, the whole world will know. The coming of our Lord is the climax of history. It is the triumph of the kingdom of God over the forces of hell. It is the climax of the great controversy between good and evil.

The aged apostle John, a prisoner on the rocky, barren Patmos, joyfully wrote, "Behold, He is coming with clouds, and every eye will see Him" (Revelation 1:7). Separated from his family, friends, and fellow Christians, John longed to see the One whom his soul loved. He longed for the day when he could sing with the redeemed of all ages, " 'Blessing and honor and glory and power be to Him who sits on the throne, and to the Lamb, forever and ever!' " (Revelation 5:13). This is prophecy's big picture.

The prophecies of Daniel and Revelation focus on much more than cryptic symbols, bloodthirsty beasts, dreadful dragons, and the antichrist's mark. They speak of a climax of all things. They speak of Jesus and His everlasting kingdom. In Revelation 7, John looks beyond all of earth's coming sorrows to this magnificent scene: " 'Therefore they are before the throne of God, and serve Him day and night in His temple. And He who sits on the throne will dwell among them' " (verse 15).

We have within us a God-shaped vacuum that will never be filled unless God fills it. Our hearts cry out for intimacy with the Creator. We long for God. Since the day Adam and Eve sinned, humanity has felt a sense of loss, an emptiness within. The only thing that can fill this aching void is the reality of God's presence. When Jesus returns, this longing will be fulfilled. The kingdom of God will be restored. The entire universe will sing. There is nothing quiet or silent about this event. This is the coronation of a King! The entire universe shouts His praise! Revelation's prophecy of the seven trumpets concludes with these words: " 'The kingdoms of this world have become the kingdoms of our Lord and of His Christ, and He shall reign forever and ever!' " (Revelation 11:15).

As in the book of Daniel, the prophecies of Revelation graphically describe the destruction of all evil forces at the coming of our Lord. John pictures God's "sickle" destroying all sin and sinners (see Revelation 14:19, 20). In the glorious triumph of the coming of our Lord portrayed in Revelation 19, John sees heaven open. Jesus Christ, symbolized as a conquering general riding a white horse, returns. All the evil forces that stand in His way are destroyed. The powers of hell that battle against His kingdom are doomed. The "beast," the "false prophet," and all those who oppose, oppress, and persecute God's people are "cast alive into the lake of fire burning with brimstone" (Revelation 19:20). And Jesus is exalted as "KING OF KINGS AND LORD OF LORDS" (verse 16).

In Revelation 20, John depicts a desolate earth with Satan bound and the wicked destroyed for one thousand years (see verses 1–3). During this thousand years, which some Bible students term the "millennium," the redeemed or saved have been caught up to meet Christ in the air at His return (see John 14:1–3; 1 Thessalonians 4:16, 17), and they reign with Jesus in heaven (see Revelation 20:4). As heaven's books are opened, the saved see clearly that in His love, God has done everything possible to save every single person.

At the conclusion of the thousand years, the Holy City descends from heaven to earth, the wicked dead are resurrected, and Satan leads these legions of the lost to attack the Holy City (see Revelation 20:5, 7–9). Then the cleansing fire of God's presence descends from heaven and devours sin and sinners forever, purifying the earth.

John tells us what follows: "I heard a loud voice from heaven saying, 'Behold, the tabernacle of God is with men, and He will dwell with them, and they shall be His people. God Himself will be with them and be their God. And God will wipe away every tear from their eyes; there shall be no more death, nor sorrow, nor crying. There shall be no more pain, for the former things have passed away' " (Revelation 21:3, 4).

What a hope! What a destiny! What a bright picture of tomorrow! Beyond our heartaches, sorrow, and tears, Jesus will come. Beyond the disasters of tribulation, Jesus will come. He won't come secretly, or silently. He will come as King of kings. He will come as Lord of lords. He will come as the mighty Conqueror. He will come to reign eternally, and the whole world will know it!

The End-Time Jesus

For the past two thousand years, Jesus has been the center of controversy. Many are willing to accept Him as a divine teacher, a wise rabbi, a compassionate healer, or even a spectacular miracle worker. But the divine Son of God offering eternal life to all humankind? Never.

Here is precisely where the problem lies: Jesus claimed to be divine.

Jesus applied to Himself an Old Testament expression that refers to·God. At the flaming bush, God identified Himself to Moses as the "I AM"—the self-existent One, the One who has no beginning or end (see Exodus 3:14). Jesus made the claim to be God by taking that name. He said, " 'Most assuredly, I say to you, before Abraham was, I AM' " (John 8:58). Those who heard Jesus say this knew exactly what He meant. John wrote in the next verse, "Then they took up stones to throw at Him." Those people were so infuriated that Jesus would claim divinity that they tried to kill Him.

Here is the bottom line. You can't have it both ways. Either Jesus was divine or He wasn't. If He wasn't, then He was a liar or self-deluded. Can you in all honesty say that Jesus was a good man who taught the highest moral teachings and lovingly ministered to each person He met but was dishonest or delusional regarding His own identity? It just doesn't make sense. Either Jesus was who He said He was or He wasn't. If He was not, He certainly wasn't a good man, a moral teacher, or a compassionate healer. Good men don't lie. Moral teachers don't pervert the truth. Compassionate healers don't deceive multitudes.

However, the controversy regarding Jesus' identity still rages today. The devil doesn't mind if people diminish Jesus, considering Him merely a moral teacher. There are thousands of good teachers who impart wisdom. The devil doesn't care if people accept Jesus as the most compassionate man ever. The devil doesn't care if people accept Jesus as a role model for healers. The devil hates one thing—when people accept Jesus as the Messiah, as the Savior and Lord of their life.

Recently, some unusual challenges to Jesus' identity have arisen. The evil one recognizes that if he can mislead people regarding who Jesus really is, he can destroy the entire Christian faith. If Jesus isn't divine, His offer of eternal life is false. If Jesus isn't divine, He has no power to forgive sin. If He isn't divine, He certainly can't raise the dead. If He isn't divine, the credibility of the entire New Testament crumbles. This is why the devil will do everything he can in every way he can to destroy our confidence in Jesus.

Misinformation in the popular media

Dan Brown's *The Da Vinci Code* has captured the attention of millions of people internationally. Its sales are off the charts. It has run through one bestseller list after another. More than fifty million copies of the book have been sold. And Hollywood's version of the story has been released in theaters around the world, drawing huge crowds. The central theme of Brown's story challenges Jesus' divinity. This fictitious mystery suggests that a secret code supposedly hidden in the works of Leonardo da Vinci claims that Jesus was married to Mary Magdalene and a royal line of the so-called "sacred feminine" descended from their daughter still exists in Europe.

The book makes numerous other erroneous claims. It claims that Jesus wasn't divine and that the church began to proclaim His divinity only after a very close vote of the Council of Nicaea in A.D. 325.

This claim is preposterous. The Council of Nicaea did consider the issue of the divinity of Christ. Heresy had arisen in the early Christian church. A group called the Arians had challenged the historic position of the church that Christ was the divine Son of God. The church council reaffirmed the church's well-established position with a resounding vote in favor of Christ's divinity: 316 for and only 2 against. This was hardly a close vote! And the two bishops who voted against the divinity statement were part of a heretical group from Egypt.

The Da Vinci Code also claims the Bible has evolved through countless translations, editions, and revisions. It asserts that history has never had a definitive version of the Book. Supposedly, the Emperor Constantine was responsible for formulating the New Testament canon as we know it today.

However, before accepting a book as inspired by God, early believers asked a number of probing questions.

- Is this writing an eyewitness account of the life of Christ? If not, does it harmonize with eyewitness accounts?
- Does the work agree with previous revelation in the Old Testament? Or does it contradict what God has already revealed?
- Does the book reveal the life-changing power of God?
- Was the book accepted as divinely inspired by the people of God to whom it was given?

Numerous ancient manuscripts contain the Gospels. The Chester Beatty papyrus p^{45} dates to the third century and contains portions of the four Gospels and the book of Acts. The Bodmer papyrus p^{66} (A.D. 200) contains the Gospel of John. The Bodmer papyrus p^{75}, dated to the early third century, contains the Gospels of Luke and John. The Syriac version of the New Testament can be traced back to the second and third centuries. And the Coptic version of the New Testament dates to the third century as well. All of these manuscripts of the New Testament were in existence before the Council of Nicaea and the time of Constantine, when the New Testament was supposedly formulated. Dan Brown claims his work is historical fiction—in other words, that while the story is fictitious, the historical facts are true. However, his book might better be called "fictitious fables." It is an incredibly biased view in which the author clearly distorts historical facts.

Early believers were absolutely convinced Jesus Christ was the divine Son of God. People don't put their life on the line for a myth. In about A.D. 105, the early Christian leader Ignatius declared, "God Himself was manifested in human form." In about A.D. 150, Clement of Alexandria, Egypt added, "It is fitting that you should think of Jesus Christ as God." And in about A.D. 160, Justin Martyr said, "The first begotten word of God is even God."

In the Bible's last book, Revelation, Jesus appears to the aged apostle John exiled on the Isle of Patmos and says, " 'Do not be afraid; I am the First and the Last. I am He who lives, and was dead, and behold, I am alive forevermore. Amen. And I have the keys of Hades and of Death' " (Revelation 1:17, 18). In this passage, Jesus identifies Himself as the eternal Son of God. He is the One who once lived on earth and is now alive forevermore. The grave couldn't hold Him. Death couldn't shackle the Life-Giver. Christ is divine. He has risen from the tomb.

The devil hates this truth, and in these last days, he has done everything he can to distort it. One of his strategies is to discredit the Word of God. Recently the *National Geographic* magazine published a manuscript titled "The Gospel of Judas." This so-called gospel portrays Judas dramatically differently than do the eyewitness accounts of Matthew, Mark, Luke, and

John. In the Gospel of Judas, the betrayer becomes a collaborator. Supposedly, Jesus and Judas agree that Judas will betray Jesus. Judas becomes a hero. He assists Jesus in fulfilling the divine plan. This is totally opposite of the biblical account.

Here are some facts to keep in mind. The media tend to be "anti-Christian." They have a secular bias. Often they will publish stories that tend to be one-sided, casting Christianity in a dubious light. The Gospel of Judas discovered in Egypt and bought recently on the antiquities market was not written by Judas. It is not an original work. It is a copy of a copy of a copy. It has been dated by scholarly specialists as coming from the fourth century A.D. Although the original was written much earlier, it was considered heretical by the early church leaders.

In *Adversus haereses (Against Heresies),* the early church leader Irenaeus refers to "an unspeakable number of apocryphal and spurious writings, which they themselves [heretics] had forged to bewilder the mind of the foolish" (Irenaeus, *Adversus haereses,* 1.20.1). This early church historian then warns that the Gospel of Judas is a deceptive heresy.

For the past two thousand years, the devil has been attempting to undermine our faith in the Word of God and cast doubt on who Jesus is. The apostle Peter reassures us of the certainty of our faith with these telling words, "We did not follow cunningly devised fables when we made known to you the power and coming of our Lord Jesus Christ, but were eyewitnesses of His majesty" (2 Peter 1:16).

Let's suppose that in the twenty-first century, someone wrote a history of America that denied the eyewitness accounts and historical records of the Founding Fathers. Let's suppose this new version of history contradicted the written words of Benjamin Franklin, George Washington, and Thomas Jefferson. What would you say? You'd say this new-fangled history is impossible. Eyewitness accounts are the most reliable.

The Gospel of Judas is another of the devil's deceptions. If you read it carefully, you'll find that it too reflects the early Christian heresy of the Gnostics. The Gnostics believed that everything material was evil. In their view, God couldn't become a man because His body would be evil. They taught Jesus was a spiritual being who never really died or rose from the dead. The Gospel of John addresses this heresy in 1 John 4:2, 3: "By this you know the Spirit of God: Every spirit that confesses that Jesus Christ has come in the flesh is of God, and every spirit that does not confess that Jesus Christ has come in the flesh is not of God."

Jesus was really born. He really lived. He really died. He really rose from the dead. He really ascended to heaven. He is really coming again.

Jesus is a real Savior who forgives our sins and brings peace to our hearts, hope to our souls, courage to our lives, and power to make us whole.

Christ's life-changing power

A number of years ago, I was conducting an evangelistic series in an eastern city. Our meetings were held at the civic center. After one of the meetings, a skeptic approached me, wanting to argue. Now, I don't mind honest questions, but I'm not interested in debating with people whose minds are already made up. This fellow was quite aggressive. Waving his finger, he continued to move toward me. He argued that Christ was merely a good man; certainly not divine. His arguments continued. He wanted to engage in a verbal sparring match. He was hoping to show off his supposed brilliance to the people standing next to me.

I had just preached, and I was tired and in no mood to argue. Standing next to me was my friend Bill. To appreciate the story, you need to know something about Bill. He is about six feet two inches tall, he weighs about two hundred pounds, and his body is a combination of Charles Atlas, Hulk Hogan, and Arnold Schwarzenegger. Bill was built! He'd been a leader of a motorcycle gang and had been in and out of trouble most of his life. Then he met Jesus one night in our meetings, and God transformed his life.

Too exhausted to argue with the scrawny skeptic, I looked at Bill and said something like this: "Take care of this guy for me. You answer his questions."

Bill looked down at the skeptic and said, "Sir, you should be glad Christ is divine. If He weren't, I'd still be in the streets robbing people like you. But Jesus has changed my life. In Christ, I am a new man."

You can never meet Christ—really meet Him—and remain the same. Even ancient secular historians who didn't believe in Him as the Messiah acknowledged His incredible power to transform lives. There are multiple references to Christ outside the Bible in the Jewish and Roman accounts of the first and second century A.D. Suetonius (c. A.D. 69–122), the chief secretary for Emperor Hadrian, had access to the Roman imperial records. Here is what he said: "He [Claudius] expelled the Jews, who had on the instigation of Chrestus [Christ] continually been causing disturbances, from Rome." From what Suetonius wrote, we can infer that many Jewish Christians were so committed to Christ as the divine Son of God that they wouldn't burn incense to Caesar and consequently were expelled from the city of Rome. Christ had so transformed their lives that they were willing to put everything on the line.

Josephus (c. A.D. 37/38–100), the greatest Jewish historian of the first century, wrote of "James, the brother of Jesus, who was called Christ." And in the early second century, the Roman Pliny the Younger wrote numerous letters to varying political and social leaders throughout the known empire. One of these letters gives us insight into what the early Christians believed about Jesus. Pliny wrote, "They [the Christians] were in the habit of meeting on a certain fixed day before it was light, when they sang in alternate verses a hymn to Christ, as to a god."

Both Jewish and Roman believers knew the authentic Christianity of the first century was based on this fundamental truth—that Jesus was genuinely the Son of God. His offer of pardon and peace was real. His offer of forgiveness and forever was real. His offer of mercy and miracles was real. His offer of grace and growth was real. His offer of happiness and hope was real.

History written in advance

Let's consider a few specific prophecies that conclusively identify Jesus as the Messiah. Most biographies are written after an individual has lived. In these prophecies, Jesus' biography was written before He was ever born. You may be thinking, *Well, it's pretty simple to figure out. Jesus just read these prophecies and then lived them. He fulfilled them because He knew them.*

It would be difficult to plan the place of your birth. Seven hundred years before Christ, the prophet Micah wrote, " 'You, Bethlehem Ephrathah, though you are little among the thousands of Judah, yet out of you shall come forth to Me the One to be ruler in Israel, whose goings forth are from of old, from everlasting' " (Micah 5:2).

What a prophecy! The eternal One, the One whose "goings forth"—His origin—have been from old, from everlasting, the Ruler in Israel—the Messiah—would be born in Bethlehem. How did Micah know centuries in advance precisely where the Messiah would be born? Jesus' parents lived in Nazareth. It was a decree of Caesar Augustus that brought them from Nazareth to Bethlehem the very night Christ was born.

The prophet Isaiah identifies Jesus' mother as a virgin (Isaiah 7:14). His family tree and lineage take Him back to the tribe of Judah (Genesis 49:10) as an heir to David's throne (Isaiah 9:7).

Many of the ancient predictions about Jesus were fulfilled in the last twenty-four hours of His life. A friend, not an enemy, would betray Him (Psalm 41:9). He would be betrayed for thirty pieces of silver

(Zechariah 11:12). He would suffer and die for the sins of His people (Isaiah 53). His enemies would pierce His hands and feet (Psalm 22:16). Not one of His bones would be broken in death (Psalm 34:20). He would be buried in a rich man's grave (Isaiah 53:9). His body would not decay in the tomb because He would miraculously rise from the dead (Psalms 16:10; 49:15).

These are just a few of the amazing predictions that confirm beyond a shadow of a doubt who Jesus really is. For inquiring minds, living in the end time, there is ample evidence to meet Satan's last-day challenge. The New Testament believers accepted the reality of who Jesus was. Believing He was divine, they gave their lives to Him. They were willing to die a cruel, martyr's death rather than give up their faith. They were transformed by the fact that they knew this divine Christ's offer of eternal life was not a myth or fable. His offer of life-transforming power was real too. These believers saw too much, they knew too much, they witnessed too much to believe anything else. They were convinced by what they experienced.

The greatest testimony of Christ's divinity is what He has done in your own life. No one can argue with how Christ has changed you. Let the witnesses from the New Testament story speak. Let the voices from the past echo in our ears. Let narratives two thousand years old come to life.

Come with me down the crowded streets of Jerusalem and meet Bartimaeus. His testimony is plain. "I once was blind but now I see." You can't convince this man that Jesus isn't all He claims to be. This once blind beggar now sees his family and friends for the first time. All of life is fresh and new.

Meet the paralytic who sat by the pool of Bethesda. After thirty-eight years in a horrible condition, he believed Christ's word, and he arose and walked. He has no question who Jesus is!

Meet a penniless woman who hemorrhaged constantly for twelve years. Exhausted, weak, poor, out of money, desperate, she touched the hem of Jesus' garment and was instantly healed. New life flows through her veins. Ask her, and she will tell you, "He changed my life!"

Why not interview Jairus, a wealthy, aristocratic Jewish executive? When his only daughter—a lovely twelve-year-old—died, he knew where to turn. Is Christ divine? Is He all He claims to be? You can't convince Jairus of anything else after his dead daughter rose from her deathbed and ran into her daddy's arms. And you can't convince Mary and Martha that Jesus is not all He claimed to be when through their tears they saw Lazarus arise from the grave after being dead for four days.

Here's the point of every miracle in the New Testament: When you know Jesus, really know Him, He changes your life. You can never meet Christ and be the same again. You can never meet Him without being radically changed. You can never encounter Christ without Him influencing your life forever.

Jesus is the center of end-time living. Without Him, you can't face the coming Tribulation successfully. In Him, our future is secure.

Hope Beyond Katrina

Her name was Katrina, but she was no lady. She is no more, but the images of the lives she shattered, the homes she destroyed, the cities she leveled, and the families she devastated will be etched in our memories for a long, long time. We see her fury in the 135-mile-per-hour winds that lashed the ocean into 20-foot swells that battered the Louisiana coastline. We see her rage in the block after block, street after street, neighborhood after neighborhood, town after town destroyed. From Biloxi to Gulfport to New Orleans, Katrina littered her debris across the once beautiful landscape. Alabama, Mississippi, and Louisiana experienced her wrath.

Like a boxer throwing a knockout punch, she hit the New Orleans levees hard. Water from Lake Pont-chartrain burst through them and inundated the city. We saw Katrina's hand in waterlogged shops, swamped streets, and flooded houses. More than a thousand people were killed by the fury of the storm. Thousands of families were separated. Experts estimate the area suffered property loss amounting to thirty billion dollars. It will take years to rebuild the coastline.

Then, just as we were drying out from Katrina and a few people were straggling back into New Orleans to rebuild their shattered lives, Katrina's twin sister Rita proudly announced her arrival. She slammed into the Texas coastline packing winds of 125 miles per hour and causing 1 million people to flee from Galveston to Houston. In 2005 for the first time in history, the weather service, which names the season's storms from A to Z, had more storms than letters.

Something has gone terribly wrong. Nature is doing strange things these days. Floods ravish China. A tsunami devastates Southeast Asia. Typhoons wreak havoc in Indonesia. Hurricanes rip apart the southern United States. Weather patterns dramatically change, and we all are left wondering what in the world is really going on? Where is our planet headed? Is what we see merely a freak of nature or is there something going on behind the scenes? Is some evil power sinisterly plotting to destroy our world? Who can hold back the winds? Who can stop the rains? Who can halt the devastation?

In an end-time sermon recorded in the Gospel of Luke, Jesus outlined the signs that will precede His return. After discussing such things as wars, famines, pestilences, and rising crime and violence, Jesus mentioned a cluster of incredible omens in the natural world. Our Lord said there would be " 'distress of nations, with perplexity, the sea and the waves roaring; men's hearts failing them from fear and the expecta-

tion of those things which are coming on the earth' "
(Luke 21:25, 26).

Jesus' prediction was amazingly accurate. Natural disasters are increasing at alarming rates. The 2005 Atlantic hurricane season with twenty-eight named storms was the most active season on record. And with fifteen hurricanes, the 2005 season had the most hurricanes ever recorded in one year in the United States. Since 1900, we've averaged seventeen major earthquakes (7.0–7.9 on the Richter scale) and one devastating earthquake (8.0) per year. The National Earthquake Information Center records fifty earthquakes each day, or more than eighteen thousand per year. In the decade ending in 2004, some 3,960 major natural disasters took hundreds of thousands of lives in countries around the world.

"Sudden destruction"

The words of the apostle Paul echo down the centuries. His inspired predictions are being fulfilled before our eyes. Writing with penetrating insight regarding our day, the apostle declared, "You yourselves know perfectly that the day of the Lord so comes as a thief in the night. For when they say, 'Peace and safety!' then sudden destruction comes upon them, as labor pains upon a pregnant woman. And they shall not escape" (1 Thessalonians 5:2, 3).

Natural disasters are bursting upon the world as an overwhelming surprise. "Sudden destruction" has devastated our villages, towns, and cities. Our property suffers billions of dollars' worth of damage each year. The extraordinary has become the ordinary. The occasional storm has become commonplace. What we once considered unusual has become normal.

What do you do when the ground beneath your feet is shaking? What do you do when nothing seems certain anymore? What do you do when you can lose everything in an instant? Maybe it's time to pause, take a deep breath, and evaluate what really is important. Maybe it's time to take spiritual inventory.

The apostle counseled us with these penetrating words, "You are all sons of light and sons of the day. We are not of the night nor of darkness. Therefore let us not sleep, as others do, but let us watch and be sober" (1 Thessalonians 5:5, 6). In other words, it's time to take spiritual inventory. How is your soul's health? Do you place a priority on spirituality? Is your spiritual experience superficial or shallow? Are you growing spiritually each day? Is your experience with God this year the same as it was five years ago? What changes for the better have taken place in your character this last year? Are you kinder, gentler, more understanding, and more committed? What direction is your spiritual life going? Are you moving closer to God or drifting further from Him?

Disasters call us to take a spiritual inventory. Uncertain times urgently appeal to us to place our faith in something that is certain. When everything around us seems to be crumbling, it is time for us to take our eyes off the temporary and focus on the eternal. God is still seated on His throne. Although at times it may not appear to be true, He is still in control.

A few years ago, a busy editor developed severe eye problems. Thinking he might need an operation, he visited his eye specialist. There he learned that things were not as bad as they appeared to be. The doctor told the editor that he merely needed to rest his eyes for about six months.

The editor objected. "I'll lose my job," he said.

So the doctor suggested an alternative plan. The editor's office overlooked a beautiful valley and mountain range. The doctor gave the editor a prescription for his overtaxed eyes. "Once an hour," he said, "take ten minutes off. Leave your editing and gaze out the window at the mountains. Looking into the distance will refocus your vision."

At times, we need to look into the distance to refocus our vision as well. As the simple chorus says, "Turn your eyes upon Jesus, look full in His wonderful face; and the things of earth will grow strangely dim in the light of His glory and grace."

All the challenges and hardships of life are calls to take spiritual inventory and focus on the eternal. They speak to us loudly of our need for a deeper faith. They are urgent invitations to know God for ourselves. The first lesson we learn from disaster is to take a spiritual inventory.

The second lesson disaster teaches is our need to evacuate as quickly as possible. In New Orleans, in the face of hurricane Katrina, too few people evacuated, and the death toll was far higher than it should have been. If more people had heeded the mandatory evacuation order that the local and state officials had put in place, many lives would have been saved. When hurricane Rita approached the Galveston, Texas, coastline, one million people fled.

We shouldn't flirt with disaster by comfortably staying put in the face of danger. Some situations that we face are potentially deadly. Our only safety is to flee immediately. When Joseph was tempted by the enticing allurements of a married woman, he fled. The Bible graphically describes the scene in these words: "She [Potiphar's wife] caught him by his garment, saying, 'Lie with me.' But he left his garment in her hand, and fled and ran outside" (Genesis 39:12). Joseph knew that unless he fled immediately, he would fall to the treacherous wiles of the temptress. Her beauty would have overwhelmed him. Similarly, in the days of Lot, Sodom and Gomorrah were a cesspool of sin. Dark clouds of doom hovered over the cities. The judgments of God were about to fall. And God's message to Lot was plain: "Escape for your life." You cannot play with sin. It is destructive.

Disaster's third lesson is this: Go to higher ground. Storms do most of their devastation in low-lying areas. As the storms of difficulty approach at the end time, God calls us to seek higher ground. The lower the level of your spiritual life, the more devastating the winds of temptation are. The higher the quality of your spiritual life, the easier it is to deal with temptations. God calls us to "take another step toward Me. Seek higher ground." An old hymn puts it this way: "I'm pressing on the upward way, new heights I'm gaining every day. . . . A higher plane than I have found; Lord, plant my feet on higher ground."

Christianity is not static. It is dynamic. God calls us from the lowlands of temptation where the winds of satanic enticements destroy our souls to the heights of His marvelous grace, the joys of His abundant love, and the companionship of His glorious presence.

You can live a vibrant life during the end time if you see the storms of life as an opportunity to "come up higher"; to grow spiritually. Trials and obstacles are God's call to higher, holier living. They are God's invitations to know Him more intimately and to love Him more fully. I don't mean that God sends these difficulties. He doesn't. The devil is on a leash, but sometimes God gives him a rather long leash. Satan can bring disaster only as far as God allows. When disaster strikes, God uses it to accomplish His ultimate purpose of revealing the temporary nature of life and the fragility of all material things.

The divine presence

Calamities become opportunities to know God better. They become doorways to deeper faith. They become divine invitations to find refuge in Him. During the challenges he faced, David, the psalmist, found refuge in God. In the storms of life, he found security there. More than forty times in his psalms he described God as his place of refuge from the disasters that threatened to destroy him. In his times of trouble, he sang God's praises. "I will sing of your strength, in the morning I will sing of your love; for you are my fortress, my refuge in times of trouble" (Psalm 59:16, NIV). In the presence of Christ, there is peace. And He is present amidst the storms of life.

Trisha lived in low-income housing in New Orleans. A few months before Katrina struck, Trisha became a committed Christian and began attending one of New Orleans' inner-city churches.

Fearful of leaving the city, Trisha decided to stay put during the hurricane. She was one of only two people left in her apartment building. And although she had no electricity and was running low on food, she survived the storm quite well—quite well, that is, until looters ransacked the building. She heard the screams of women being dragged into the complex and raped. At first, she barricaded herself in her apartment, locked her doors, and prayed. Then she realized that she must leave quickly or face devastating consequences. But she had a major problem. Her car was sitting in three feet of water, and she was low on gas. Of course, there were no mechanics available to help her get her waterlogged car started, and no gas stations were open.

Trisha prayed, "Oh Lord, You are my refuge and security. Help me, Jesus. Help me now." Then, rushing to her car, she nervously stuck the key in the ignition. When she turned the ignition switch, the car sputtered. The exhaust began spitting out water. Trisha quickly shifted into drive, and to her absolute amazement, her car plowed through the flooded streets! It was as if some divine hand was guiding her.

Trisha glanced nervously at the gas gauge. It read empty. But a calm assurance flooded her soul. It was as if God was saying, "I am in control here. Don't worry; just keep driving." And she did. She drove sixty miles to Baton Rouge, Louisiana, to safety. Somehow, in the midst of incredible disaster, God was there. He was there, encouraging His child to hang on, to find in Him refuge and security. He was lifting Trisha's spirits in spite of her terrible situation. He was still guiding her in her troubles.

In the devastating storms of your life today, God is there. He still whispers, "Peace, be still." He still holds you in His arms and says, "Everything is going to be all right." He still invites you to place all of your anxieties in His hands.

Shortly after the devastation of hurricane Katrina, one Federal Emergency Management Agency (FEMA) official commented, "Since the 9/11 disaster, the United States government has spent billions on an emergency response system for national disasters, but Katrina was just too catastrophic." The only unfailing emergency response system is Jesus. He never lets us down in the emergencies we face. He is never caught by surprise. No catastrophe is ever too great. Jesus is never short of resources to cope with disaster. All of heaven's resources are available for you. Ten thousand times ten thousand angels are at His command.

There is nothing your heavenly Father wouldn't do for you. His love for you is unending. In fact, He loves you so much that Jesus is coming back for you soon to take you to a land where disasters will never touch you again. The storms of life will be over then. Catastrophes that unexpectedly snuff out thousands of lives and destroy billions of dollars' worth of property in an instant will be a thing of the past.

In God's love, we find refuge during all of today's trials, and hope for an unending tomorrow filled with the joy of His presence.

What Difference Does Faith Make?

In the early 1970s, my wife and I lived at a small mission training school in Wildwood, Georgia. I was responsible for teaching a group of about thirty students how to tell people about Jesus and His offer of eternal life, and I often traveled on dirt roads into the backcountry of the Georgia hills to study the Bible with families who lived there.

One day, I was sitting at a table in a simple log home, sharing God's Word, when the door opened and a man smoking a big cigar walked in. With a booming voice, he exclaimed to all of us, "Praise God, I am healed! Praise God, I am healed!" He then explained that at a recent medical appointment, the doctor had told him that he had lung cancer. Now he had been examined again, and there was no trace of cancer.

I couldn't refrain from asking, "What about your cigar?"

The man responded, "No problem. When God heals you, He does it completely. You can smoke cigars as long as you want. When you have enough faith, that's all that counts."

Do you agree with the big-cigar man? If you have enough faith, can you go right on smoking cigars even though they cause cancer? Will your faith counteract the toxic, cancer-producing effects of the cigar?

Jesus predicted faith would be in short supply at the end time. He asked this probing question: " 'When the Son of Man comes, will He really find faith on the earth?' " (Luke 18:8). Evidently, genuine biblical faith will be difficult to find before the coming of Jesus.

Most of us would agree that God won't heal us of cancer so we can return to doing the thing that caused it. You can have all the faith in the world, but if you attempt to run across six lanes of traffic speeding down the Interstate at sixty-five miles per hour, you're likely to be hit. And if you smoke cigars, you may develop lung cancer.

So, what is faith? How does it work? Is it some kind of divine rabbit's foot or four-leaf clover that guarantees that when people just "name it" and "claim it," they'll get what they want? Is it some kind of psyched-up positive thinking that solves all a person's problems? Why does it seem to work wonders for some people and do little for others?

God defines faith

Scripture contains one entire chapter devoted to faith. It's Hebrews 11. This chapter clarifies some of life's deepest issues. It answers some of life's most fundamental questions. It cuts to the heart of how to live our lives. Here God lists the heroes of faith down through the ages—people whose names hang high in heaven's hall of fame.

Verse 1 of this chapter serves as an introduction to what follows. It defines faith as "the substance of things hoped for, the evidence of things not seen." Faith is the "substance . . ." *Sub* means "under." We have words like *"sub*marine" ("under the sea") and *"sub*terranean" ("under the earth"). Literally, a "substance" is something that "stands under." It is the essence of a thing—what it is. It supports or sustains something. It is a foundation.

So, faith is the quality that supports us when all of life falls apart. Faith stands under everything else. Faith sustains us in the perplexing questions of life. It is the essence of the spiritual life; it is what keeps it from crumbling.

However, biblical faith produces some surprising results. On the surface, it's rather confusing—a casual look at Hebrews 11 will leave you with more questions than answers. Follow me as we take a brief journey through this chapter.

- **Verse 4:** Abel's faith is so strong that it gets him killed. If he didn't have faith, he would have lived.
- **Verse 5:** Enoch's faith takes him to a place where he will never die. If he didn't have faith, he would have died.
- **Verse 7:** Noah's faith leads him to stay where he

is for 120 years and build an ark. Noah obeys God and stays on his God-given task.

- **Verse 8:** Abraham's faith leads him to leave the place where he is, to go where God directs him. Abraham obeys God and leaves home.
- **Verse 21:** Joseph's faith leads him to remain in Egypt, and God entrusts him with unusual wealth.
- **Verse 23:** Moses' faith leads him to leave Egypt and live in poverty in the wilderness.
- **Verse 30:** By faith the walls of Jericho fall down and the Israelites preserve their lives in battle.
- **Verse 32:** By faith mighty Samson brings walls down and loses his life.
- **Verses 34, 35:** By faith God's people are protected and miraculously delivered from death by the sword.
- **Verses 36, 37:** By faith God's people hang on despite persecution and are killed by the sword.

Do you catch what's going on here? The contrasts leap off the pages of this classic chapter on faith. By faith Abel dies and Enoch lives. By faith Noah stays and Abraham goes. By faith Joseph remains in Egypt and becomes rich and Moses leaves Egypt and becomes poor. By faith some are delivered from the sword and others are slain by it.

What is the common thread? In each instance, it is faith—trusting God enough to believe His promises and do just what He says. The heroes in God's hall of fame had different experiences, but they all trusted

God. They trusted Him in life and in death. They trusted Him when He commanded them to stay and when He commanded them to go. They trusted Him when they lived in poverty and when they rejoiced in wealth. They trusted Him in sorrow and in joy.

The essence of faith is trusting God. It is believing that He loves us and knows what is for our good. Abel, Enoch, Noah, Abraham, Jacob, Joseph, Moses, and the other heroes of Hebrews 11 had one thing in common: *faith,* a faith that sustained and supported them throughout their lives. They lived lives of faith.

What difference does faith make in our lives? " 'The just shall live by faith' " (Romans 1:17). Faith is not simply belief or mental assent; it is something we live by.

Faith as relationship

Faith is a relationship with God as with a well-known friend—a relationship that leads us to do whatever He asks and accepts whatever He allows to happen to us. Faith believes God will strengthen us to triumph over every difficulty and overcome every obstacle until the day we receive our final reward in His eternal kingdom.

Faith energizes. It enlivens. It lifts our spirits. It encourages our hearts. It renews our hope. It lifts our vision.

Faith believes God's power and receives God's gifts before they are realized. To *receive* the gift and to *realize* the gift are two different things. To receive the gift is to accept it in advance, believing that God will give it if and when we need it. To realize it is to experience its actual presence.

Faith is active, not passive. It is believing exactly what God says and acting upon it. It is living a life of trust.

Faith is Abel offering his sacrifice.

Faith is Enoch walking with God.

Faith is Noah building the boat.

Faith is Job, afflicted head to toe with boils, crying out, "Though He slay me, yet will I trust Him."

Faith is Abraham saying goodbye and leaving home. It also is Abraham offering up Isaac as a sacrifice.

Faith is Jacob believing in his wayward sons and blessing them in death.

Faith is Joseph betrayed by his brothers, sold into slavery, lied about by Potiphar's wife, cast into prison, and still trusting God.

Faith is Moses forsaking the pleasures of Egypt.

Faith is Joshua marching around Jericho.

Faith is Daniel, a captive in a foreign land, trusting that God has a purpose for his life.

Faith is Jesus dying on the cross, with blood running down His face, crying out in triumph, "Father, into Your hands I commend My spirit."

Faith is Paul shipwrecked, beaten, stoned, whipped, and imprisoned, confidently declaring, "I know whom I have believed."

Faith is filled with hope and optimism because it trusts God. It believes God always has the good of His children in mind. "For he who comes to God must believe that He is, and that He is a rewarder of those who diligently seek Him" (Hebrews 11:6).

Faith is trusting God for strength in our weakness, wisdom in our ignorance, courage in our fear, peace in our anxiety, hope in our despair, guidance in our doubt, and joy in our sorrow.

Faith doesn't know defeat. It doesn't understand the word *impossible.* It is filled with courage.

People of faith trust God enough to act upon His Word, believing He'll give them the strength to do whatever He asks them to do. Faith is the key ingredient for end-time living.

What has God asked you to do? What journey of faith has He asked you to take? What pilgrimage has He asked you to make? Faith is trusting God on the journey—trusting that He is leading you through life.

Where we can obtain faith

Faith always has a source. It isn't faith in oneself or faith in faith. It isn't some kind of hyped-up positive thinking. It isn't a self-centered ego trip. It is faith *in God.*

And God is always the source of our faith. Faith is the gift He gives us as we trust in Him.

Moses' faith enabled him to endure because he saw Him who is invisible (see Hebrews 11:27). How do you see something that is invisible? You must see it by faith.

Faith grasps the reality of God's presence. Dietrich Bonhoeffer, a humble, godly pastor, was thrown into prison during World War II. Allied planes raided the German city nearby, and the prison shook under the intense bombing. Of that time Pastor Bonhoeffer wrote, "I sensed the presence of God." Awaiting death in a German prison camp, this godly man sensed God's closeness by faith. He had learned to trust God with his life.

To understand faith fully, we must also understand what faith is not. Faith is not sight. The apostle Paul stated it eloquently when he said, "We walk by faith, not by sight" (2 Corinthians 5:7). If you can see the answer to your prayers before you pray, you don't need faith.

When you've prayed for the five hundred dollars you need to pay your bills this month, it's much easier to sing God's praises after you receive the money than before. It is far easier to thank God for healing you of cancer than to trust Him when you are going through chemotherapy. It isn't difficult to be joyful when your marriage problems are solved. It is much more difficult to trust when you are going through them. Faith trusts God before the problem is solved. It sees beyond the difficulties and challenges of life to a loving God who will work them out in His way and in His time.

Faith isn't sight, nor is it understanding. A very dear friend of my wife and me, Sandy Wyman Johnson, shared this powerful scriptural insight with me. Sandy's son Trevor died in childhood after a lengthy battle with leukemia. Trevor was a delightful child whose faith encouraged his mom greatly. When we were talking about Trevor's death one day, Sandy quoted Philippians 4:7, "The peace of God, which surpasses all understanding, will guard your hearts and minds through Christ Jesus." She then made this telling observation: "Mark, when your mind does not understand, you still can trust."

Sandy is right. You don't have to understand everything God is doing in order to trust that what He is doing is right. God's ways are far beyond my understanding. Faith is trusting that God knows what He is doing when I don't.

Faith isn't sight. It isn't understanding. And it isn't selfishness disguised as belief. Faith doesn't focus on what I want; it focuses on what God wants. Jesus illustrated faith at its best when He prayed in Gethsemane, " 'Not as I will, but as You will' " (Matthew 26:39). Faith always seeks the Father's will.

Have you heard the story of the five-year-old girl whose daddy overheard her praying for a pink elephant? Her daddy slipped into her room and knelt quietly beside her. When she finished praying, he asked, "Honey, where will you keep the pink elephant if Jesus gives you one?"

"Oh!" she said, "we'll keep it in your room, Daddy."

"Who will feed it?"

"You and Mommy can, Daddy."

"Now, honey," Daddy softly said, "who will clean up after it? Elephants make pretty big messes."

"Daddy, you can buy a shovel!"

Do you think God sent the girl a pink elephant in answer to her prayer?

Have you ever prayed for a pink elephant? Are your prayers merely petitions to get from God what you want? Or is prayer a time when you open your heart to God to discover what He wants?

We can become so absorbed in what we want God to do for us that we fail to receive what He wants to give us. Faith isn't believing that because I prayed, the sun will shine today so I can take my family to the beach. Faith is trusting that whether or not it shines, God is going to give me a wonderful day. Faith isn't believing that God must heal me when I demand Him to. It is committing my life to bring glory to God no matter what happens in my life. Faith is always directed to God. It is God-centered.

Have you ever wondered what to do when your faith is small? Have you wished you had a great deal more faith? I have good news for you. You have more faith than you realize. The problem isn't that you don't have any faith. The problem is that you haven't exercised the faith you have. The apostle Paul speaks of God having "dealt to each one a measure of faith" (Romans 12:3). When you accepted Jesus, God placed a measure of faith within your heart. And when you exercise the faith that God has given you, your faith grows. Ellen White, one of my favorite authors, said, "Your faith must not let go of the promises of God, if you do not see or feel the immediate answer to your prayer. Be not afraid to trust God."[1]

Her husband's killers

One of the past century's most amazing stories of faith is the story of Elizabeth Elliott. Elizabeth's husband, Jim, was speared to death by Auca Indians on January 3, 1956, on the Curaray River in Ecuador. Some considered the Aucas to be the most savage tribe on earth. Jim was part of a mission group that wanted to teach this primitive tribe about the God who loves us. Along with five others, he made repeated attempts to contact them.

To assure the Aucas of their good will, the mission group flew over their village and dropped gifts from the air. All seemed to be going well. The barriers seemed to be breaking down. The missionaries felt it was safe to approach them. They landed their small plane on a narrow sandbar by the river and set up base camp. Every day for several days they radioed their wives at a mission station to report their progress. Then there was silence. The men no longer made the radio calls that their wives expected. For five long days of uncertainty, these five women and their children waited to find out what had happened. Then the terrible truth was discovered.

During the time of uncertainty, Elizabeth Elliott wrote the following lines in a letter to her parents: "I want you to know that your prayers are being answered moment by moment regarding me. I am ever so conscious of the everlasting arms. I have no idea what I will do for Him if Jim is dead, but the Lord knows I am at rest."

When word came out that all five were dead, the women and children gathered to comfort one another and to pray. One of the women went to the piano and began to play the song they had all sung together the morning the men left on their journey. "We rest on Thee, our shield and defender. We go not forth alone against the foe. Strong in Thy strength, safe in Thy keeping, tender . . . we rest on Thee and in Thy name we go."

Elizabeth Elliott committed her life in faith to communicate to the Aucas the love of God and the life available through Christ. Within a few years, God had miraculously opened the door to reaching them, and this amazing woman of faith entered the Auca village and lived among them. She wrote, "Faith must embrace doubt. Nothing less than faith could have brought us to Auca land." God opened the door to one of the most savage tribes on earth.

Now, fast-forward. It is a sunny day in the Ecuadorian jungles. The sky is blue; the sun bright on the lush landscape. Time has passed. The Aucas have accepted the gospel. One of their own has become a Christian pastor. Now he steps into a river to baptize Rachel Saint. Years before, this man had speared Rachel's father to death on the banks of this same river. Now, faith had triumphed. It had reached out and clasped the hand of God in crisis. It had become a channel through which God's power had reached the Aucas.

Would you like to open your heart to God and by faith receive His power today? Faith is trusting God as a friend well known. This is why faith is an indispensable part of end-time living. With God's gift of faith, you will survive and even thrive in life's difficulties today, tomorrow, and in the tumultuous days ahead.

---

1. Ellen G. White, *Testimonies for the Church* (Mountain View, Calif.: Pacific Press®, 1948), 1:120.

Prayer in a Time of Crisis

It was one of the most significant turning points of World War II. Hitler's bombers were pounding the Allied positions. Defeat seemed certain. It appeared that there was no way the Allied forces would survive.

The lowland countries of Belgium and the Netherlands had fallen, Hitler's forces were pushing their way across France, and now, the narrow beaches of Belgium and France were lined with hundreds of thousands of Allied troops who had no place to go. They were trapped between the German army and the English Channel. Winston Churchill's radio address gave a grim report of the dire situation. "Ladies and gentlemen," he said, "the lights across Europe have gone out tonight."

Then something remarkable happened—something that even today, historians have a difficult time explaining. Hitler ordered his tank divisions to halt for refueling and resupply. This was incredibly odd. They had faced little opposition from the retreating English forces.

When the fog on the English Channel lifted, Churchill took advantage of the opportunity. He ordered the famed evacuation of Dunkirk. The English leader sent everything that floated across the 22 mile-wide channel and evacuated nearly 340,000 Allied soldiers from the beaches of France. When doom seemed certain in the dark days of the war, God worked a miracle.

How did it all happen? What was behind the story of one of the most outstanding rescues in English history?

Here is the untold story. For weeks before the evacuation, the lights in country churches were on all up and down the English Channel. Pastors called their members to prayer. And they came! They came by the tens, twenties, hundreds, and thousands. They prayed, and God answered. They interceded for a miracle that would change the tide of human history.

British pubs closed for prayer meetings at noon and in the evening. Schools paused frequently for a moment of prayer. Through a mighty movement of intercession, all of history was changed.

Fast-forward forty-five years to 1989. The tide of freedom was flowing across Eastern Europe. The winds of change were blowing throughout the communist states. Totalitarian regimes were crumbling like sand castles battered by the waves. Nation after nation was choosing freedom.

One of the most autocratic of all the governments in Eastern Europe was Eric Honnecker's East Germany. Honnecker ruled East Germany with an iron fist. His government exercised authoritarian control over its citizens. The details of the average person's life were carefully regulated.

In 1985, a group of Christians from a church in Leipzig, Germany, began a prayer movement. At first, their numbers were small; five or ten people met on Monday evenings. But as the months went by, their numbers grew. On a Monday night in 1989, a hundred thousand people met in churches throughout Leipzig. The prayer movement spread like wildfire across Germany until five hundred thousand and then more than one million people were praying.

One crisp October evening in East Berlin, a group of these people who were praying marched fearlessly through the streets to the Berlin Wall. To the guards' absolute amazement and horror, thousands of praying people approached the Wall. The guards seemed powerless to halt this human tide that was grasping for freedom.

Writing about this event later, the editor of the *New Republic* magazine, which is not known for its religious leanings, made a comment to this effect: "There is an old adage that says prayer changes things. We cannot vouch for the veracity of prayer, but we do know that praying people changed the course of modern Europe." Prayer makes a difference in a time of crisis.

Like pictures from the air

One thing is certain. Intercessory prayer is biblical. We may not know exactly how it works. We may not understand it completely. But merely because we don't understand something doesn't mean it isn't true.

Let me give you an example. Do you know that the air in your house is full of little pictures? If you have a box with a glass screen and if that box is plugged into electrical power, you can push some buttons on a little thing called a remote, and the pictures floating around in your house will appear on the glass screen on that box!

Although you may not understand everything about television images, that doesn't keep you from watching your favorite programs, right? You may not understand everything about electrical engineering, but that doesn't stop you from turning on the lights.

Prayer is like that. You don't have to know everything about it to benefit from it. The fact that something is infinite doesn't mean you can't know anything about it. It means that no matter how much you know about it, there is more to learn.

The apostle Paul was imprisoned in a dark, dingy, dismal dungeon in Rome. But writing to the Ephesians, he said, "I also . . . do not cease to give thanks for you, making mention of you in my prayers" (Ephesians 1:15, 16).

Paul had spent a year and half in Ephesus. Now that he was a prisoner of the Roman government and

was being held in the Mamertine Prison, he was thinking about his friends in Ephesus. So, he got down on
his knees and prayed, "Dear Lord, remember my
friends in Ephesus. Touch their lives. Give the church
members there courage and hope. Lift their spirits. In-
spire their hearts."

Paul believed in intercessory prayer. He believed
the Romans could chain his body, but they couldn't
chain his prayers. They could put him in prison, but
his prayers would still ascend beyond his cell to the
throne of God.

Paul didn't believe that prayer was merely some
kind of psychotherapy meant only to make him feel
better. He believed prayer was a path to the throne of
God. He believed that when he prayed, God would
work miracles that He wouldn't work if no one
prayed.

The believers at Colossae were also on Paul's heart.
He wrote, "We give thanks to the God and Father of
our Lord Jesus Christ, *praying always for you*" (Colos-
sians 1:3, emphasis supplied).

Verse 9 tells what the apostle was praying about:
"We . . . ask that you may be filled with the knowl-
edge of His [God's] will in all wisdom and spiritual
understanding." In effect, he was saying, "I'm praying
that you will know God's will. I'm praying that you
will make good decisions in your life. I'm praying that
you will have wisdom. I'm praying that you will grow
in grace. I'm praying that your heart will not be hard
to the gospel. I'm praying that the Spirit of God will
surround you with a hedge of protection."

It's a wonderful thing to have a friend praying for you. It's a wonderful thing to have a husband or wife praying for you. It's a wonderful thing to have a son or daughter praying for you. It's a wonderful thing to know that someone cares enough to pray for you. But these thoughts raise some questions. Isn't God already doing everything He can to bless my life whether or not someone else is praying for me? Isn't God already doing everything He can to bless our families whether or not we pray for them? Do our prayers make any difference at all, or do they just make us feel good? Are they merely some kind of mental exercise in positive thinking? Isn't God going to do what He wants whether or not we pray?

The universe-wide battle

The Bible provides clear answers. It tells us that good and evil, Christ and Satan, good angels and evil angels are battling each other. The Bible's last book, Revelation, describes the battle this way: "Michael and His angels fought with the dragon [Satan] . . . and his angels" (Revelation 12:7). One-third of the angels in heaven rebelled against God (see verse 4; cp. Revelation 1:20). Then God threw Satan and the other evil angels out of heaven, and they ended up on earth (see Revelation 12:8, 9). So, we are caught in this conflict between good and evil. The forces of evil bring disappointment, disaster, disease, and death, while the forces of righteousness bring joy and life.

In this universe-wide conflict between God and Satan, God voluntarily limits Himself. He doesn't violate our power of choice. God is allowing the conflict to play out for a time that in the light of eternity is relatively short. He wants the whole universe to see that sin ultimately brings suffering and death.

God is doing everything He can within the ground rules of the conflict between good and evil to save all humanity. Whether or not I pray, He is reaching out to my family members. Whether or not they pray for me, He is reaching out to me. Whether or not I pray, God provides a measure of protection by angelic beings.

But when we pray and seek Him, we open up new channels through which God can, in the context of the conflict between good and evil, do things that He wouldn't otherwise do. God not only respects the power of choice for people who are not praying, *He respects our power of choice as we pray.* As we pray, God pours out His Spirit through us. Prayer enables the illimitable God to help those in need.

The Bible contains many passages that encourage us to pray. It contains promises such as " 'Ask, and it will be given to you; seek, and you will find; knock, and it will be opened to you' " (Matthew 7:7). But a marvelous passage in the little letter called 1 John does more than urge us to pray. It actually explains why prayer is so effective.

The passage says, "Now this is the confidence that we have in Him, that if we ask anything according to His will, He hears us. And if we know that He hears us, whatever we ask, we know that we have the petitions that we have asked of Him. If anyone sees his brother sinning a sin which does not lead to death, he will ask, and He will give him life for those who commit sin not leading to death" (1 John 5:14–16).

The apostle John declared, "Now this is confidence that we have in Him . . ." (verse 14). Where is our confidence? *In Him!* Our confidence is not in our prayers. Our confidence is not in our faith. *Our confidence is in Him.* When we pray a prayer of intercession, we are to say, "Lord, my confidence is in You. I can't meet my own needs, but You can."

The apostle continues that the confidence we are to have in Jesus is that "if we ask anything according to His will, *He hears us."* Then John says, "If we know"— not "we guess," *"we know"*—"that He hears us, whatever we ask, we know that we have the petitions that *we have asked of Him"!*

Wonderful promise! What confidence we can have in God!

But there's more. Verse 16 tells us what happens when we intercede. "If anyone sees his brother sinning a sin which does not lead to death . . ." The sin that leads to death is the unpardonable sin. It is to rebel so completely that one's heart has become hardened to the point where one no longer hears or responds to God.

John continues about this person who sees someone else sinning, "He will ask . . ." Who is the "he" who is doing the asking? The intercessor. And what happens? "He [God] will give him [the intercessor] *life for those who commit sin not leading to death."*

In other words, God pours out His life through us to touch the life of someone else. We are the channels through which God pours out His illimitable power. Intercessory prayer *does* make a difference.

In the medical community, attitudes toward prayer are changing. A growing number of physicians believe prayer makes a difference in physical healing. More than 140 studies on religion and health have been published. Many of them were on prayer and healing. A significant number of these studies showed a positive relationship between prayer and improved health.

Dr. Randolph Byrd, a San Francisco cardiologist, selected a group of patients who had been through coronary bypass surgery. He divided them into two groups, those who were being prayed for and those who weren't. This was a double-blind study: None of the patients in the study knew who was being prayed for. People's minds can't influence their bodies by sending positive mental messages if they don't even know that someone is praying for them—which negates the criticism that the influence of positive thinking skewed the results.

Dr. Byrd distributed the names of about half of the patients to Christians who committed to pray for them. The results were remarkable. The prayed-for group healed more quickly. They needed less medication. They had less complication in healing. The non-prayed-for group made more visits to their doctor. They had more complications healing. They needed more medication, and they had more infection.

Intercessory prayer is powerful. It makes a difference. It makes a difference in the lives of those who are praying, and it makes a difference in the lives of the people for whom they are praying.

Jesus' prayer life

Jesus regularly slipped off to a quiet place to pray. He sought God for strength to meet the challenges of the day. He pled with His Father for strength to overcome Satan's temptations. The Gospel of Mark informs us about one of Jesus' early morning prayer sessions this way: "Now in the morning, having risen a long while before daylight, He went out and departed to a solitary place; and there He prayed" (Mark 1:35).

Jesus recognized the inner spiritual strength that comes through prayer. His prayer life was a priority. Luke's Gospel records, "So He Himself [Jesus] often withdrew into the wilderness and prayed" (Luke 5:16). Prayer was not something Jesus did occasionally. It was a vital part of His life. His prayer life renewed His experience with God. It gave Him courage and strength to face temptation. Jesus came from these prayer sessions with a freshness and deepened commitment to doing the Father's will.

If Jesus, the divine Son of God, needed time in His Father's presence to overcome the fierce temptations of Satan, how much more do we need time in God's presence! We will come forth from these times alone with God filled with faith. Our courage will be revived. Our spiritual strength will be increased. Prayer will intensify our desire to do God's will.

One thing is sure. We can't face the devil in our own strength. Nor can we expect our children to go out into the world to meet the foe on their own. Prayer is the answer. When we pray, God bathes us with His presence and power. When we pray, He touches the hearts of our loved ones. Prayer is vital to facing the enemy successfully during the end time.

We can't live godly lives during the end time if our prayer life is spasmodic. When our connection with God is broken, our power from Him is cut off. When there is little prayer, there is little power. Prayer is our humble acknowledgment that we can't live the Christian life without His strength. It is the admission of our inability to cope with Satan's temptations alone. Through prayer, we are more than able to handle Satan's temptations. The devil is no match for the trusting child of God who, through prayer, has laid hold of divine strength.

When we've gone onto our knees and pled with God, we will see God's hand move in miraculous ways. As Jesus did, we will come from these seasons of prayer refreshed and invigorated. We will also sense that God is working through our prayers to transform the lives of others.

Many years ago, a godly Christian woman invited her husband to attend a revival meeting with her. The man was not a Christian. He vehemently opposed anything to do with Christianity, and he wouldn't even consider her invitation. Rather than attend the meeting, the man left home for the weekend to go hunting.

Deeply disappointed, his wife shared the experience with her pastor. Together, they interceded for this unbelieving husband.

On Saturday night, the preacher made an appeal to those present in the meeting who had not yet committed their life to Christ. He asked them to come to the front of the church, where he would lead them in a prayer of commitment to Christ. Imagine how shocked the Christian woman was when she saw her husband walk down the aisle from the back of the church to make that commitment. She hadn't even known he was at the meeting. He'd slipped into the back of the church without her seeing him.

After the meeting, he told her this story. Friday night, he'd tossed and turned in his bed. He'd hardly slept all night. He was troubled. Something just wasn't right. He felt that he was a lost man. He knew he had to make things right with God. Hunting no longer mattered. His beer no longer mattered. His ego no longer mattered. What did matter was being free from guilt and finding peace with God. The man drove directly to the church for one reason. He was ready to commit his life to Christ. The intercessory prayer of a godly wife made a huge difference in this man's life.

Praying parents can make an incredible difference in the lives of their children. Praying spouses can make an amazing difference in their marriage. Praying church members can make a huge difference in their church. Praying families can make an enormous difference in their neighborhood. Praying students can change their school. The legacy of such spiritual giants as Joseph, Moses, and Daniel demonstrates that praying people change the course of history.

Do you want to be an end-time world changer? Bathe your life in prayer. Cover your family with prayer. Saturate your neighborhood with prayer. Intercede for your spouse, your children, your friends, and your work associates.

Lift up your petitions to the God who hears. Seek the One whose ear is always bent low listening for the requests of His children. Open your heart to a Savior who is more interested in answering your prayers than you are in praying. When you do, you will discover a vital secret for living a successful Christian life during the end time.

When Wounds Won't Heal

A few years ago, two of my friends lost their seventeen-year-old son in a tragic car accident. It was a horrible, heart-breaking experience. A fuel truck raced through an intersection and rammed into his car, setting it aflame, and the boy burned to death. The wounds from that terrible experience still linger in his parents' minds.

A middle-aged woman attending one of my evangelistic meetings in a Midwestern city was stabbed nearly seventy times by her mentally deranged husband in a fit of rage. Miraculously, she survived. The physical wounds have healed, but the deeper emotional ones remain.

Another couple I know lost their first child while it was still in the mother's womb. One day she didn't feel the baby's movement anymore. She was almost full term; her obstetrician had to induce labor and take her through the birth process. Her anguish was almost unbearable, and wounds remain.

What do you do when the hurts of the past remain? How do you move on when painful memories haunt you? How do you forget a wound that is ever present? One thing is for certain—all attempts to heal ourselves will fail. Our world is littered with the emotional wrecks of desperate people trying to ease their pain. Some have sought relief in drugs and alcohol. Others have consumed themselves in their work or material possessions. Many people have drowned themselves in the endless pursuit of pleasure. They have attempted to get as many thrills out of life as possible, hoping to ease their pain.

However, people's frantic attempts to do more, have more, acquire more, have left them empty. Too often, the result is broken hearts and broken homes. Depression and divorce are often the twins of wounds that don't heal. Chemical solutions, the antidepressants of the twenty-first century, may provide some temporary relief, but their long-term effectiveness is highly questionable.

There must be a better way, and there is. It is called grace—God's grace.

The grace that a loving heavenly Father in mercy extends from the Cross when we fail is a healing grace. The grace that provides power to live godly Christian lives is a healing grace. The grace that daily provides life's "good things" is a healing grace.

In a moment of intense emotional pain, the psalmist David cried out, "Have mercy on me, O LORD, for I am weak; O LORD, heal me, for my bones are troubled. My soul also is greatly troubled" (Psalm 6:2, 3).

David recognized that there is no source of lasting healing apart from our Lord's healing grace. The prophet Hosea adds, "He will heal us; . . . He will bind us up" (Hosea 6:1).

Generally, healing takes time. It is a process. God does not heal us all at once. His healing takes place gradually. In the healing journey on which He leads us, we are drawn closer to Him daily. As we kneel before Him in prayer, His healing grace flows into our hearts. As we open His Word, His precious promises become heaven's medicine to bind up our emotional wounds.

We must recognize two things: The deeper the wound, the more time it takes to heal. And some people heal quickly, while others heal more slowly. When you have a physical wound, you can hasten the healing process. Dressing the wound daily with antiseptics and healing ointments and taking antibiotics to prevent infection helps. By following three biblical principles, you can also speed the healing of your emotional wounds.

1. You must refocus the past.

We won't heal now unless we refocus the past. Healing doesn't occur when we deny the past. It doesn't take place when we pretend the past doesn't exist. It occurs when we accept by faith that although bad things happen to good people, God is bigger than all the pain of our past.

We may have caused our emotional pain because of our own misguided actions. Or our pain may result from choices others have made—choices beyond our control. Some people are victims of rape or abuse. Others are victims of a car accident that didn't result from their negligence but from a drunk driver's addictive habit. Still others have suffered a painful divorce due to a spouse's infidelity.

The issue here is not who caused what. The events happened. They are a reality. Accept that fact. Look beyond what happened to the God of comfort and healing who is still there. The apostle Paul has pointed us to "the Father of mercies and God of all comfort, who comforts us in all of our tribulation, that we may be able to comfort those who are in any trouble, with the comfort with which we ourselves are comforted by God" (2 Corinthians 1:3, 4).

God doesn't wave a magic wand and erase our past. He comforts us in our deepest pain so we can comfort others who hurt. He applies healing ointment to our bleeding hearts so we can apply it to the hearts of others who bleed. He soothes our pain so we can soothe others' pain.

Healing from our pain doesn't mean we deny what happened to us. It means we refocus what happened. Whatever it was, we don't try to figure it out, because in most instances we can't. So, we move beyond asking the question "Why did this happen to me?" to accepting by faith that God is still here and that in ways we can't understand, He has our welfare in view.

The apostle Paul was shipwrecked, beaten, unjustly condemned, imprisoned, exiled, and sentenced to death. Yet he confidently proclaimed, "We know that all things work together for good to those who love God, to those who are the called according to His purpose" (Romans 8:28). Notice that the apostle doesn't say that all things are good. Numerous things that are not at all good happen in life. They are evil. They bruise us. They bring us grief. But even in these difficult challenges, God is present, working out all things for our good.

In the magnificent tapestry of our life, God is weaving a pattern that will be visible only in eternity. Looking back from eternity's perspective, we will understand His hidden purposes. Only then will the mysteries of life be made plain. When we understand this, even when we are overwhelmed with sorrow because of some vicious attack of the enemy, we can still say with the apostle Paul, "The Lord will deliver me from every evil work and preserve me for His heavenly kingdom. To Him be glory forever and ever. Amen!" (2 Timothy 4:18).

God gave me a living example of His ability to "deliver us from every evil work" and "preserve us for His heavenly kingdom." I met Joan Herman for the first time in 1963 as a college student. She left an indelible impression upon my life. In 1948, while still in her late teens, Joanie developed bulbar polio. Eventually, she became paralyzed from the neck down. She couldn't dress or feed herself. An attendant had to brush her teeth, button her blouse, comb her hair, and perform numerous other routine tasks for her.

For twenty years, Joanie spent most of her time in an iron lung. But here is the amazing thing: She remained buoyant through it all. She radiated God's love and goodness. My wife and I visited Joanie numerous times in the hospital. We went to encourage her, but we always left feeling encouraged ourselves. God's strength was revealed in her weakness.

Joan Herman developed a life-changing ministry from her hospital bed. She constantly interfaced with hospital administration as a patient advocate to improve the quality of her hospital friends' lives. She also initiated a Bible class for patients in a New Britain, Connecticut, hospital for the handicapped. They came to class in wheelchairs and on crutches. They came with their walkers and canes. Some were wheeled in on their beds.

From a hospital bed in a small room in southern Connecticut, this paralyzed woman exerted an influence that reached the highest levels of society. She made an impact on countless lives. Why? She was able to refocus her energies on a God who could take the great tragedy of her life and turn it into an opportunity for service to others who, like her, had suffered loss. Tragedy made Joan Herman better, not bitter. It didn't rob her of the opportunity to serve; it provided her that opportunity. It didn't prevent her from discovering meaning in life; it was the doorway to it.

You can speed up the process of healing from emotional pain if you can see God as dramatically greater and more powerful than anything that has ever happened to you. If, in the context of your tragedy, you can find the opportunity to minister to others, you'll have discovered the key to unlocking the door of wholeness. Healing occurs in the present when we re-focus the past.

There is a second eternal principle of emotional healing.

2. You must forgive those who wounded you.

You can heal in the present only if you forgive those who wounded you in the past. If you cannot forgive, you cannot heal. Jesus has already carried our grief and sorrow to the cross.

If anyone has ever been treated unjustly, it was Jesus. He didn't desire to be crucified. He was innocent. Yet He was rejected, despised, and mocked. He was betrayed and beaten. He was condemned and crucified. His friends forsook Him. His chosen people rejected Him, and the Romans cruelly crucified Him.

The pain we bear pales in comparison to the pain He bore. His suffering was as much more intense than ours as His righteousness and goodness are greater than ours. Yet on the cross Jesus prayed, " 'Father, forgive them, for they do not know what they do' " (Luke 23:34). He forgave those who crucified Him, and His forgiveness embraces the whole world.

Have you been treated unfairly? Have people close to you forsaken you? Have you been deeply hurt by those you loved? If you have, you can understand a little of how Jesus felt and the pain He endured. Yet He forgave. His love reached out to the very ones who treated Him so cruelly. It is at His cross that we find the strength to forgive others. If the righteous Son of

God forgave those who wounded Him, we too can forgive others who wound us.

Sometimes forgiveness shows up in the most unusual places. Kim Phue's story brought home to Americans the horror of war. Nick Ut of the Associated Press photographed her running down a road in South Vietnam naked, terrified, screaming in pain, just after a bombing attack.

Shortly after Nick snapped the picture, he took Kim to the hospital. Years of painful burn therapy followed. Then, after the war, Kim enrolled in Saigon University to become a doctor. But she was more valuable to the communists as a propaganda tool. When government officials discovered that Kim was the little girl whose picture had been featured in newspapers and magazines internationally via the Associated Press, they pulled her out of school and assigned her to a government office where she could tell the story of American brutality.

However, in 1986, the Vietnamese government sent Kim on a goodwill mission to Cuba. There she met Bui Huy Toan, a committed evangelical Christian. As their relationship grew, Bui shared with Kim the power of the gospel. Kim was amazed at Christ's love for and forgiveness of His enemies. Charmed by Christ's grace, Kim committed her life to Him. Then, in 1992, she and Bui were married, and on their way home from their honeymoon in Moscow, they defected to Canada.

Since then, Kim has shared the story of her conversion with thousands of battle-hardened soldiers. At a

Veteran's Day service in 1996, she laid a wreath at the Vietnam Memorial in Washington, D.C. She told the assembled Vietnam vets, "As you know, I am the little girl who was running to escape the napalm fire. I have suffered a lot from both physical and emotional pain. Sometimes I thought I could not live, but God saved my life and gave me faith and hope." Kim then publicly forgave the pilot who dropped the napalm bomb that seared her skin and killed her grandmother and two younger brothers.

Many of the veterans gathered at the memorial that day began to weep. They sensed that Kim was genuine. She had no bitterness. Her forgiveness of the ones who caused her so much pain came from the heart. She understood the meaning of the Cross.

Kim Phue was able to forgive the soldiers who nearly destroyed her life and caused her lifelong pain because she had experienced Christ's forgiveness herself. We forgive because we've been forgiven.

Many Christians misunderstand what it means to forgive someone who has hurt them deeply. Commonly, people have two misconceptions regarding forgiveness. Some people think that forgiving someone who has wronged them will justify the hurtful behavior. They have the idea that forgiveness means acceptance of wrongdoing. Other people think they needn't forgive the person who wronged them until that person repents of the wrongdoing and asks for forgiveness.

Did Christ condone the behavior of His crucifiers by forgiving them? Did He justify their sinful acts by praying "Father, forgive them"? Certainly not! Forgiveness doesn't declare that what the offender did is right. Forgiveness releases the offender from our condemnation because Christ has released us from His condemnation. Christ's love flows through us, giving us grace to be free from the poison of bitterness.

In Jesus' parable, forgiveness was in the heart of the father long before the prodigal returned home. The son couldn't receive his father's forgiveness until he repented of his sinful lifestyle. But the father's forgiving heart longed for his son to return before the boy ever took the first step toward home.

God's heart overflows with forgiveness toward His wayward children. Although it is true that we can't receive God's forgiveness until we confess our sins, our confession doesn't create forgiveness in God's heart. It is there all the time.

You can't heal the hurts of the past unless you allow God to place His forgiveness in your heart today. Your receiving God's forgiveness doesn't depend on the actions of someone else. If someone hurt you in the past and you still are filled with resentment, you are allowing that person to destroy your present. It is far better to forgive and forget than to remember and resent. It is far better to let God's grace heal your heart and then to move on with your life than it is to nurse your emotional wounds and be stuck in the past.

The apostle Paul put it well when he encouraged us to "be kind to one another, tenderhearted, forgiving one another, just as God in Christ forgave you" (Ephesians 4:32).

Jesus can heal our brokenness only if we're willing to forgive those who did the damage to us in the first place.

Sometimes people find it more difficult to forgive themselves than anyone else. We may be hurting because we know we're responsible for the pain of others. These wounds from the past will heal only when we've repented of the wrong we did, confessed to the people we've injured, and done what we could to make things right. Then we must allow Jesus to forgive us—and we must forgive ourselves. If the infinite God, the Holy One of Israel, can forgive us, then we should accept that forgiveness and let go of our feelings of guilt.

There is one final aspect of emotional healing I would like to share with you.

3. You must live in the blessings of the present.

You can heal the wounds of the past only if you live in the blessings of the present. You must let the goodness of God today fill the brokenness of the past.

The story of Job reveals this eternal principle. Through no fault of his own, Job lost his home, his job, his family, his friends, and his health. His life was dramatically changed in a few short days. But Job didn't curse God. In faith he cried out, " 'I know that my Redeemer lives, and He shall stand at last on the earth; and after my skin is destroyed, this I know, that in my flesh I shall see God' " (Job 19:25, 26).

In the challenges of his life, Job looked to God. Although he didn't understand what was happening to him or why it was happening, he lived a life of trust. When he summed up what he'd learned about God, he began with these words: " 'I know that You can do everything' " (Job 42:2). Job's faith despite adversity opened the door for God to work some amazing miracles on his behalf.

A lack of faith limits God. Our heavenly Father longs to do more—much more—than we could ever imagine. The Bible gives us this incredible testimony regarding Job: "The LORD restored Job's losses" (verse 10); "the LORD blessed the latter days of Job more than his beginning" (verse 12); "Job died, old and full of days" (verse 17). Job learned to live in the blessings of the present.

An old Chinese woman came to a very wise old sage and shared her sorrows with him. Through her sobs, she asked, "Why have I been so cursed? Why is my sorrow so great?"

The sage responded, "Find a home that sorrow has not touched, and ask them the secret of happiness."

Two weeks later, the woman returned. "Sir, I am so blessed," she said. "There is no home that sorrow has not touched. I have so much to be thankful for."

The giants of faith in Scripture saw God's hand working in their lives in the present, but they all looked beyond to a glorious tomorrow where sorrow would never touch their lives again. Abraham "waited for the city . . . whose builder and maker is God" (Hebrews 11:10). Paul realized that he had "fought the good fight" and confidently said, "There is laid up for me the crown of righteousness" (2 Timothy 4:7, 8).

James counseled, "Blessed is the man who endures temptation; for . . . he will receive the crown of life" (James 1:12). Peter proclaimed, "We, according to His promise, look for new heavens and a new earth" (2 Peter 3:13). The aged apostle John, exiled to the lonely Isle of Patmos, writes of a God who " 'will wipe away every tear from their eyes' "! He encourages us to look forward to an eternity where " 'there shall be no more death, nor sorrow, nor crying. There shall be no more pain, for the former things have passed away' " (Revelation 21:4).

Secure in the presence of Jesus, our wounds will finally be healed. Our pain will be gone forever. He will wipe away our tears with the tender touch of His love. The past will be gone forever. It will never haunt us again. Our painful memories will be gone. The abundance of heaven's grace will salve our deepest hurts. We will delight in the presence of Jesus forever, and for us that will be more than enough recompense.

End-Time Survival Strategies

It is God's Word, the Bible, that reveals Christ. It is God's Word that strengthens our faith. It is His Word that unfolds truth. It is His Word that exposes error. It is His Word that prepares us for Satan's fiercest temptations. God reveals Himself through His Word. That is why Satan hates it. That is why all the powers of hell want to destroy it.

God's Word reveals survival strategies for end-time living. It shows us clearly how to thrive in life's toughest times. Bible characters discovered these principles and lived by them in the face of persecution, imprisonment, and death.

If anyone was caught in the midst of the titanic struggle between the forces of good and evil, it was the apostle Paul. He shared eternal truths that will enable us to stand fast in the worst of times. They are the apostle's "attitudes of being." They bolstered his faith. They encouraged his heart. They lifted his spirit in the challenges of life. All the demons of hell cannot destroy the humble child of God who embraces these principles. They are timeless and life-changing.

Live a life of trust

We find the first eternal truth in Paul's letter to the Corinthians: "Not that we are sufficient of ourselves to think of anything as being from ourselves, but our sufficiency is from God" (2 Corinthians 3:5). *Principle #1: To stand fast in the worst of times, we must trust God.* Where there is no trust, there is no spiritual strength. Left on our own, we are totally incapable of battling the evil one.

We are not sufficient; God is. Our sufficiency is from Him. The Christian life from beginning to end is one of trust and dependence, not one of self-sufficiency. We lose faith when we feel sufficient on our own. The less sufficient we feel, the more we must trust God—and the stronger we become.

- Our righteousness is not sufficient to save us; His is. "It is God who justifies" (Romans 8:33).
- Our strength is not sufficient to deliver us; His is. "The Lord knows how to deliver the godly" (2 Peter 2:9).
- Our good works are not sufficient to sanctify us; His are. " 'I am the LORD who sanctifies them' " (Ezekiel 20:12).
- Our power is not sufficient to resurrect our bodies; His is. " 'I am the resurrection and the life' " (John 11:25).

- We cannot make ourselves immortal; He can. " 'I give them eternal life' " (John 10:28).

Throughout life, our inadequacy is Christ's sufficiency. At times, we all cry out from the depth of our being, "I'm too weak to cope with life's challenges. I'm incapable of facing the devil's temptations. I'm unable to handle my daily pressures. I am just not sufficient for all the stressors that are rapidly coming at me all at once." In all our circumstances, God is our sufficiency.

- When we have stress at work, God is our sufficiency.
- When there are problems in our families, God is our sufficiency.
- When we have health problems, God is our sufficiency.
- When we have financial problems, God is our sufficiency.
- When we care for elderly parents, God is our sufficiency.
- When we cope with loneliness, God is our sufficiency.
- When we are challenged at school, God is our sufficiency.
- When we feel insufficient, incapable, and inadequate, God is our sufficiency.

Professor Marilyn Hellenburg certainly discovered this principle of trusting absolutely when she felt inadequate. Marilyn taught English at Kearny State College. One semester, to begin class, she had all the students write statements about themselves. Here is what one student, Ka Yeung Kwan, wrote: "I think English is a real bore. My main hobby is harassing stupid teachers and English teachers are the stupidest of all."

The natural response to a comment like this is either to become defensive or to withdraw emotionally from the individual completely. Throughout the initial class period, Kwan snickered, mumbled under his breath, dropped books on the floor, and squirmed in his seat. He was extremely disruptive. That night Marilyn, a committed Christian, acknowledged before God that she was incapable of dealing with the problem. She sought Christ's sufficiency.

While she prayed, she was impressed to see Christ in Kwan. How? He was not even a Christian. She continued to ask Christ for His sufficiency to meet this challenge.

In the following weeks, Kwan often yawned conspicuously in class and made comments about how boring the class was. To upset Marilyn, he sprinkled his first essay with obscene language. He also monopolized classroom discussions by arguing with other students.

One day, Marilyn read a poem in class titled *Outwitted*, by Edwin Markham. Before she read it, she said, "This poem is dedicated to Kwan." The poem says,

He drew a circle which shut me out—
Heretic, rebel, a thing to flout.
But Love and I had the wit to win:
We drew a circle that took him in!

After class one day, Kwan asked, "Why don't you just give up on me?" Then he confided, "You can't let people get too close to you. I play a game in which I try to hurt them before they hurt me. I've been rejected so many times that I can't stand it anymore."

On his final essay, Kwan wrote these words: "There are three kinds of teachers: Those who are interesting but stupid; those who are intelligent but boring; those who are both boring and stupid, like my English teacher." When Marilyn read it, tears came to her eyes. She felt all of her efforts had failed. Then she prayed, "Jesus, be my sufficiency. I have invested so much energy in this young man, I am emotionally drained."

When Marilyn handed Kwan's paper back, she began to cry and simply commented, "Kwan, I can't play emotional mind games. You matter to me. I care for you as a person. I am concerned." Then she walked away.

While she was sitting in her office and crying, Kwan walked in and placed a note in her hand. It read: "I am sorry I hurt you. No one has ever cared for me before. If this has something to do with your Christ, I want to know Him too."

In all of life's inadequacies, we must trust. The more incapable we feel, the more we need to trust. The more inadequate our sufficiency, the more we need His sufficiency. The gates of hell will not destroy the child of God who hangs on in simple trust. Christ is our sufficiency, so trust.

Live a life of courage

Now we come to the second in the trinity of survival attitudes the apostle Paul offers us. His first-century words speak to a generation living in the twenty-first century. They were important then, but they are much more important now. Here are his hopeful words: "Since we have this ministry, as we have received mercy, we do not lose heart. . . . We are hard pressed on every side, yet not crushed; we are perplexed, but not in despair; persecuted, but not forsaken; struck down, but not destroyed" (2 Corinthians 4:1, 8, 9).

In other words, all the stressors and pressures of life didn't cause him—and needn't cause us—to become discouraged. *Principle #2: To stand fast in the worst of times, we must hang on to our courage.* In Christ, we can have a confident, positive attitude. Christ's grace enables us to cope with all of life's unbearable stressors.

What did the apostle mean when he said, "We are perplexed"? Certainly, even for him, life contained its share of unanswered questions. There are many things we simply cannot understand, but that need not destroy our faith. What we do know is far more significant than what we don't know. The One who has changed our heart is more important than the unanswered questions in our mind.

We may be perplexed, pressed or stressed, and even persecuted, but we need not lose heart. Here's why: "Even though our outward man is perishing, yet the inward man is being renewed day by day" (2 Corinthians 4:16).

The great heroes of faith lived lives of incredible moral courage: Joseph didn't lose heart when his brothers betrayed him. Moses didn't lose heart wandering in the wilderness. Elisha didn't lose heart when thousands of enemy soldiers surrounded him. Daniel didn't lose heart despite being a captive in a foreign land. Jeremiah didn't lose heart though he was martyred. Peter didn't lose heart even when he was condemned by the guilt of his sin in denying his Lord. And though stoned, shipwrecked, and imprisoned, the apostle Paul didn't lose heart.

We can avoid losing heart only if our "inward man" is being renewed day by day. When God's people Israel wandered in the wilderness, manna fell from heaven each day to supply their needs. God provided their daily food. Each morning, except on the Sabbath, the Israelites gathered the manna. God gave them sufficient for that day. If they missed gathering it each morning, they went hungry.

Every heart holds a hidden hunger to know God. This inner longing can be satisfied in only one way. Jesus said, " 'This is eternal life, that they may know You, the only true God, and Jesus Christ whom You have sent' " (John 17:3). We get to know God through His Word, the Bible. God offers us nourishment in His Word. But like the manna, today's supply is inadequate for tomorrow. We must "eat" it every day.

There is one prime way to build strong faith; one way to build courage; one way not to avoid losing heart: *We must live in the presence of God.* Robert Wong lived in the presence of God, even in a communist prison. His inner person was renewed every day. He was in solitary confinement for four years. He was imprisoned or in labor camps for fifteen years. During much of that time, his family wasn't allowed to visit him, and his letters home were restricted to only one hundred Chinese characters a month.

Robert remembered that the hymn "Give Me the Bible" was number 115 in the Chinese hymnal. He wrote "hymn 115" in one of his letters home. When his mother received the letter, she puzzled over that cryptic line until she concluded that Robert was trying to tell her that he wanted a copy of the Bible. At this time, the authorities were allowing Robert's family to visit him monthly. When family members visited their imprisoned relatives, they often brought large bars of soap for them. Mrs. Wong hollowed out one of these large bars of homemade soap and carefully concealed a small New Testament in it.

That Bible, the precious Book of God, sustained Robert for days, weeks, and months. He drew courage from its pages. His inner person was renewed day after day. Heroes of faith down through the centuries have drawn courage from God's Word. That's how they have not lost heart.

Corrie Ten Boom tells the story of a financial crisis in her father's watch-making shop. She kept the books and knew they hadn't received enough money to pay the bills. Then an extremely wealthy businessman entered the shop and looked at one of the most expensive watches. After examining it, he decided to buy it. He gave Corrie's father, Mr. Ten Boom, the money.

In passing, he said, "I want to buy this watch because I have a very expensive one that just doesn't work. I took it to a young watchmaker in town, but he couldn't do anything with it."

"May I see the watch?" Mr. Ten Boon inquired. In a moment, he had it running perfectly. Mr. Ten Boon then said, "You won't be needing this new watch; yours will work just fine now," and he returned the man's money.

Corrie overheard the conversation, and her heart sank to her feet. Immediately, she "lost heart." Her courage ran away like a dog running from its master. When the potential customer left, she exclaimed, "Papa, how could you? You know how much we needed the money!" Her father replied, "Corrie, have courage. Trust in the Lord."

- In the presence of the Lord, our courage is renewed.
- In the presence of the Lord, our strength is restored.
- In the presence of the Lord, our faith is revived.
- In the presence of the Lord, our hope is rekindled.

Live a life of hope and joy

Paul concluded his thoughts on end-time living with these words: "We do not look at the things which are seen, but at the things which are not seen. For the things which are seen are temporary, but the things which are not seen are eternal" (2 Corinthians 4:18).

Principle #3: To stand fast in the worst of times, we must look to God's promises for the future.

As Christians, we look beyond what is to what will be. We look beyond today to tomorrow. We look beyond the night to the morning. We look beyond the present to the eternal. We look beyond our tears to joy. We look beyond sickness to health. We look beyond earthly poverty to heavenly riches. We look beyond heartache to happiness. We look beyond earth's problems to heaven's solutions. We look beyond time to eternity. We look beyond disaster to deliverance. We look not at what we see; instead, by faith, we grasp the eternal joys we cannot see.

Here, then, are the apostle Paul's end-time survival attitudes:

1. We are not sufficient—but Christ is. Live a life of trust. Dwell in the presence of God. In the difficulties of life, faith is trusting God as a friend, knowing for certain that He will never do us any harm.

2. "We do not lose heart." Live a life of courage. God beckons you into His presence for a dose of new courage. Courage is the tenacity to hang on and never give up, knowing God's strength will get you through.

3. "We do not look at the things which are seen." Live a life of hope and joy, looking to the promises of God. Vision is the ability to look beyond today to tomorrow. It is seeing the future through God's eyes. It is the ability to grasp the reality of eternity today.

God wants to give you an extra dose of faith, courage, and vision for all the challenges you face. Why not ask Him for it today?

Surviving Armageddon

Armageddon is a hot topic today. It is on the lips of preachers and politicians. Hollywood producers have used Armageddon's end-time connotation to pack theaters nationwide—the movie *Armageddon,* starring Bruce Willis, grossed more than two hundred million dollars at the box office. It is a spine-tingling drama about an attempt to save planet Earth from certain destruction. The leader of a bunch of renegade rough necks is enlisted to fly to an asteroid approaching earth with frightening speed. His task: to drill an eight-hundred-foot-deep hole and blow up the asteroid with a nuclear bomb.

The public can't seem to get enough of the Armageddon hype. Tim LaHaye and Jerry Jenkins conclude their popular Left Behind series with a book titled *Armageddon.* Their publicists spent a whopping five million dollars to promote the book.

Journalists are jumping into the act in increasing numbers. The *Washington Post* of February 23, 2003, gives us their chilling assessment of the war with Iraq: "World destabilizing aggression could spin out of control and lead to other despots arming themselves with all manner of apocalyptic weapons and perhaps to Armageddon."

A psychologist writing in the March 3, 2003, edition of *Newsweek,* just before the United States' preemptive strike on Iraq, wrote these frightening words: "The terrible consequence of an unjustified preemptive strike will turn a billion Muslims into enemies when we might have lived in peace. It will be a step toward Armageddon."

An editorial in the Syracuse, New York, *Post Standard* states, "It is not hard to fear Armageddon is near. God forgive us for what we are determined to unleash."

People use the term *Armageddon* in many ways. Economists say the bottom falling out of the economy would be an "economic Armageddon." Environmentalists talk of the deadly pollution of our atmosphere as "environmental Armageddon." Weather forecasters speak of impending natural disasters and the devastation they leave in their wake as "the force of Armageddon."

The secular press most often uses the term to denote devastation and death. However, while the popular press uses the term *Armageddon* freely, it really is a biblical term. And since the term comes from Scripture, wouldn't it be wise to return to the Bible to discover its meaning?

The subject of Armageddon is much more than discussion of a battle in the Middle East. It is more than speculation about the future. It is far more important than merely satisfying our curiosity about what is coming. Understanding the significance of Armageddon matters—it really matters—to our life today.

Armageddon is the battle of all battles. It is the mother of all wars. It is the conflict of all conflicts. It has to do with the eternal destiny of every person living on planet Earth.

Understanding the battle of Armageddon is at the heart of understanding the Bible's last book, Revelation. The aged apostle John, writing from the barren, rocky island of Patmos regarding the end time, gives us this picture of Armageddon: "Spirits of demons, performing signs, . . . go out to the kings of the earth and of the whole world, to gather them to the battle of that great day of God Almighty. . . . And they gathered them together to the place called in Hebrew, Armageddon" (Revelation 16:14, 16).

This portrayal of Armageddon comes right in the middle of ten chapters in Revelation that picture the final conflict between good and evil—the last battle between the forces of hell and the people of God. This war began in heaven. John wrote, "War broke out in heaven: Michael and His angels fought with the dragon; and the dragon and his angels fought, but they did not prevail, nor was a place found for them in heaven any longer" (Revelation 12:7, 8). The age-long controversy between Christ and Satan that began in heaven will come to its climax in the final conflict on earth. The war began in heaven thousands of years ago, but it will end on earth with the total annihilation of Satan and all of hell's evil forces.

Earth's last days

To get the picture clear in our minds, let's briefly review Revelation's portrayal of earth's last days.

- Revelation 13 describes the rise of a "beast" power—a power attempting to establish a false religion—that forces people to bear its "mark" by establishing an economic boycott, declaring that people can't buy or sell unless they have this mark of the beast.
- Revelation 14 reveals God's last message to the human race, calling all men and women to faithful obedience and urging them to worship the Creator rather than the beast.
- Revelation 15 and 16 graphically portray the pouring out of the seven last plagues and the battle of Armageddon—the battle of all battles.
- Revelation 17 reviews the prophecy of Revelation 13 and enlarges upon the conflict regarding the law of God by further attacking the union of church and state and the oppression of God's people.
- Revelation 18 forecasts the total collapse of the church/state union that comprises the beast power and repeats God's call for His people to come out of it.
- Revelation 19 vividly portrays the return of our Lord in glory.

- Revelation 20 sheds light on the millennium and God's final judgments upon Satan and his evil forces.
- Revelation 21 and 22 climaxes the entire Bible, telling of God's creation of a new heaven and a new earth. Thus, the Bible's first two chapters begin with a perfect world, and its last two chapters end with a perfect world.

If we are to understand the battle of Armageddon, we must notice the detail in the prophecy itself. Reading books about the prophecies of Armageddon will not do. Bible prophecy explains itself. Revelation's description of Armageddon answers three vitally important questions: What is the battle called? When does the battle occur? And where is the battle fought?

According to Revelation 16:14, the battle of Armageddon is called, "The battle of that great day of God Almighty." Armageddon isn't a battle between the United States and its allies and the Muslim nations. It isn't a battle fought in some desert kingdom of the Middle East. It's the universal battle between good and evil that climaxes the controversy between Christ and Satan. It's earth's last war. The forces of hell attempt to annihilate the faithful people of God forever.

According to Revelation 16:15, this battle occurs just before Jesus returns to earth. Revelation 16:16 contains a fascinating description of the battle of Armageddon that provides the master key to understanding the entire prophecy. It says, "They gathered them together to the place called in Hebrew, Armageddon."

Why did the apostle John note that the term *Armageddon* comes from Hebrew? The New Testament is written in Greek, not Hebrew. What does this Hebrew term mean?

The first part of the word is derived from the Hebrew word *Har,* which means "mountain." The second part of the word probably refers to Megiddo, a city located on the Plain of Esdraelon at the foot of Mount Carmel in northern Palestine. What actually happened on this plain? And why does God use the events that took place here as symbols in end-time prophecy?

We discover some answers in Judges 4 and 5. Jabin, a heathen king of Canaan, and Sisera, the commander of his army, oppressed Israel for twenty years. Then, through Deborah, a prophet, God called Barak to raise an army to free Israel from Jabin's power. And God enabled Israel to defeat Sisera, Jabin's army, and his "nine hundred chariots of iron." Scripture says, " 'Then the kings of Canaan fought in Taanach, by the waters of Megiddo' " (Judges 5:19). Judges 4:15 says, "And the LORD routed Sisera."

The valley of Megiddo was the place where God defeated the enemy. Armageddon speaks of victory, not victims. Its message is hopeful, not hopeless. It shouts of deliverance, not doom.

At Revelation's Armageddon, Satan marshals the legions of the lost. The apostate, fallen, corrupt religious powers unite with the secular state authorities.

Initially, an economic boycott is instituted. No one can buy or sell unless they receive the mark of the beast. Later, a death decree is enforced, condemning to death those who "keep the commandments of God and the faith of Jesus" (Revelation 14:12). A universal religio-political conglomerate is established to wipe out all faithful believers. But in the end, the battle is the Lord's. He returns to destroy the powers of hell. He triumphs over the forces of evil. The King delivers His people.

On numerous occasions in Old Testament history, it appeared there was no possible deliverance for Israel from their enemies. There seemed to be no way out. But in their moments of absolute desperation, God came through. Facing the giant Goliath and the might of the Philistine armies, David cried out, " 'the battle is the LORD's' " (1 Samuel 17:47).

When God's people faced the dreaded heathen armies, "they cried out to God in the battle. He heeded their prayer, because they put their trust in Him" (1 Chronicles 5:20). The psalmist spoke for all of us when he confidently exclaimed, "You have armed me with strength for the battle" (Psalm 18:39). In the battle we face against evil in our daily lives, we too need "the LORD strong and mighty, the LORD mighty in battle" (Psalm 24:8).

The battle of Armageddon speaks of a God who is powerful enough to crush the forces of evil. It speaks of a God who is strong and mighty—a God who has never lost a battle with Satan, and who never will lose one.

Help in the battles you face

What battle are you facing in your life today? Are you facing a struggle with some dreaded disease? Does it seem to be getting the best of you? In the end, you and God are going to win.

Are you facing a battle because of a marriage gone bad? Hang on. Don't give up. In the end, you and God are going to win.

Are you facing a battle with discouragement? Have you been "down" a lot lately? Reach out to God in faith. You and God are going to win.

Are you facing a battle with a habit or attitude you wish you could give up? Surrender to God. You and God are going to win.

At the end time, the battle will be fierce. The dragon will roar. The beast will oppress. The antichrist will persecute. But Jesus will enter the battle, and He will triumph. The prophecy of Armageddon is not a message of gloom. It is a message of encouragement. God's people do not need to live seized by fear. They can live motivated by faith.

Fear paralyzes. It cripples and immobilizes. It keeps us from living the abundant life God desires us to live. Faith, on the other hand, inspires hope. Faith lifts our spirits. Faith encourages our hearts. Revelation's prophecies predict, " 'These will make war with the Lamb, and the Lamb will overcome them, for He is Lord of lords and King of kings; and those who are with Him are called, chosen, and faithful' " (Revelation 17:14).

God is going to win. Jesus is going to defeat the dragon—Satan (see Revelation 12:9). One day Jesus will come in a blaze of glory. The righteous will be delivered and the devil defeated. The question is not whether Jesus will win; the question is whether we will be faithful.

Jesus' counsel to the church at Smyrna comes echoing down the centuries. It breathes hope into our own spiritual lives. " 'Do not fear any of those things which you are about to suffer. . . . Be faithful until death, and I will give you the crown of life" (Revelation 2:10).

Jesus gave this counsel to the church at Smyrna— now Izmir, the second largest city in Turkey. Smyrna was the home of Polycarp, a committed Christian leader in the second century who was martyred for his faith.

Polycarp was arrested on the charge of being a Christian and was ushered into the stadium amidst the turmoil and screams of the unruly crowd. They demanded his death, shouting at the authorities to throw him to the beasts.

The Roman proconsul motioned for the multitude to be quiet. Then he urged Polycarp to curse Christ. The old man stood to his full height, summoning all of the strength he could, and testified of his faith. "For eighty and six years I have served Him, and He has done me no wrong. How can I blaspheme my King who has saved me?"

Even when they burned this committed Christian martyr at the stake, he knew by faith that he was a winner, not a loser. His heart was filled with the realization that all the powers of hell couldn't destroy a child of God. One day, with the faithful of all ages, Polycarp and you and I will triumph. We are on the winning side.

The apostle John wrote, "I saw heaven opened, and behold, a white horse. And He who sat on him was called Faithful and True, and in righteousness He judges and makes war. . . . And He has on His robe and on His thigh a name written: KING OF KINGS AND LORD OF LORDS" (Revelation 19:11, 16). The rightful King of the universe will return. Evil will be vanquished. Righteousness will reign. God wins. Satan loses. Heaven triumphs. Hell is defeated.

God calls us, like Polycarp, to be faithful until He comes. This is no time for compromise. It is no time to be playing games with our faith. The call of the hour is a call to commitment—commitment so full and complete that, as the old hymn says, there is "nothing between my soul and the Savior."

Why not make this commitment today?

"It Is Finished"

In the days of the British Empire, Oliver Cromwell's secretary was dispatched to the continent on some important business. One night, he stayed in an old seaport town where the next morning he was to represent Cromwell at an important meeting. Nervously, he tossed and turned all night. He couldn't sleep.

According to an old custom, his valet slept at the foot of his bed. The secretary awakened his valet in the middle of the night, and the valet inquired what was wrong. The secretary replied, "I'm worried something might go wrong on my mission tomorrow."

"Master," said the valet, "may I ask you a question or two? Did God rule the world before you were born?"

"Most assuredly He did."

"And will He rule it after you are dead?"

"Certainly, He will."

"Then why not let Him rule it in the present too?"

The valet's words stirred the secretary's faith, and a calm assurance settled over his soul.

In moments of stress and anxiety, we too can rest in this thought. God created us. He sent His Son to redeem us, and He's coming again for us. These three realities are life-transforming. Life is not some cosmic accident. We are not playthings of chance. From Genesis, the Bible's first book, to Revelation, its last, the Bible writers celebrate life. And this life can be filled with meaning because a loving God created us in His image. Then the God of all creation, the One who made sun, moon, and stars, loved us too much to let us go when we sinned, so He sent His Son to redeem us. And now He is lonely for us and can't stand being away from us much longer, so He's coming again for us. These three encouraging truths are summed up in three words, "It is finished."

There are four significant occasions to which the Bible applies this concept. Each one has profound significance for the twenty-first century. They speak with increasing relevance to a stressed-out generation that pops antidepressants like candy.

These "It is finished" statements speak of our origin, our purpose, and our destiny. They speak of a garden called Eden, a hill called Calvary, and a city called the New Jerusalem. They speak of creation, crucifixion, and the climax of human history. They speak of self-worth, forgiveness, and deliverance.

At Creation

While the first statement doesn't contain the exact expression "It is finished," the thought is there. In writing the Creation account, Moses informs us, "Thus the heavens and the earth, and all the host of them, were finished. And on the seventh-day God ended His work which He had done" (Genesis 2:1, 2). When God completed His work of creation, He rested. In effect, He said, "It is finished."

The important point here is that creation is the work of God. We didn't create ourselves. We didn't evolve. The account in Genesis speaks of a Creator who fashioned creation Himself. Life is not a biological accident. God is the Life-Giver, the Creator, the Originator of all. And He cares for the things He has made.

You never again need to entertain the thought that you are of little value. A country-western song by a popular female vocalist goes something like this, "I want someone to notice the little things that make me who I am." The song's refrain speaks the desire of every human's heart: "More than anything, I don't want to be unknown. More than anything, I don't want to be unknown."

It's true. No one wants to be a zero. No one wants to be a cosmic orphan. No one wants to be a great big nothing.

God speaks to us personally when, speaking of Creation, Genesis says, "God ended His work which He had done." He says, "I've completed the intricate design of your being. I've fashioned the complexity of your beating heart. I've formed your life-giving cells and designed the electrical and chemical systems in your brain. I've brought together the genes and chromosomes that make you the person you are."

To place a low value on yourself is to insult the all-loving, all-powerful, all-knowing Creator who made you. The truth of Genesis speaks to our hearts today. It's the fundamental truth of life: God planned our existence and brought us each into being.

- In Psalm 33:15, the psalmist declares, "He fashions their hearts individually."
- In Isaiah 62:4, the prophet affirms, "The Lord delights in you."
- In Isaiah 43:4, God calls you "precious" and "honored."
- In Psalm 139:17, David exclaims, "How precious also are your thoughts to me, O God!"
- In Jeremiah 31:3, God says, " 'I have loved you with an everlasting love.' "
- And in Jeremiah 29:11, God joyfully assures us, "I know the thoughts that I think toward you, says the Lord, thoughts of peace and not of evil, to give you a future and a hope."

If God had a refrigerator, your picture would be on it. If God had a wallet, your photo would be in it. If God's angels could take digital pictures on their digital cameras, you would be the screensaver on His computer. If God had a cellphone, your image would be on it, and He would look at it every time He made a phone call to heavenly beings throughout the galaxy.

Aristotle said, "Man is a political animal." Thomas Wells said, "Man is a laughing animal." Ben Franklin said, "Man is a tool-making animal." Edmund Burke said, "Man is a religious animal." James Boswell said, "Man is a cooking animal." But the Bible says, "God created man in His own image" (Genesis 1:27). That makes all the difference.

Christian psychologist James Michaelson once counseled a woman who felt lonely and abandoned. As she explained how she felt, Dr. Michaelson couldn't concentrate on what she was saying because a scripture kept running through his mind: "It is He who has made us, and not we ourselves" (Psalm 100:3). This verse had no apparent connection with the woman's problem, but he couldn't stop thinking about it.

When the woman quit talking, Dr. Michaelson didn't know what to do other than to quote Psalm 100:3. So, he quietly said, "I think God wants you to know something. He has impressed my mind with this text: 'It is He who has made us, and not we ourselves.' Does this mean anything to you?"

The woman immediately broke into tears. After composing herself, she said, "I didn't tell you this, but my mother got pregnant before she was married. All my life I've felt that I was a mistake, a mere accident—that God didn't create me after all, I just happened to be. When you quoted that verse, for the first time in my life I knew God created me. I am not a mistake." This woman's perspective on life changed completely when she sensed that God crafted her in her mother's womb.

The story of the creation that has a beginning and an end speaks of a God who lovingly fashioned us individually. He is a God who considers us of immense value. To God, you are one-of-a-kind in the universe.

You are unique in all creation. You are more than skin and bones, more than a collection of cells, more than tissues, organs, and body parts. You are a unique individual created in the image of God. You are irreplaceable. There is no one else like you in the entire universe. If God loses you, there will be an emptiness in His heart forever. That's why God told Isaiah, "This people I have formed for Myself" (Isaiah 43:21).

All of heaven's attention is on you. All of heaven's power is directed for your benefit. This is the very nature of a love that is infinite. There is enough for everybody. It's like the sunshine, which shines on everyone on the beach no matter how many are there. God's love is like that. It is infinite. There's enough for all.

On the cross

We hear the second "It is finished" at the cross. The first one speaks of our worth in Christ. The second speaks of our forgiveness, acceptance, and assurance of salvation through Christ.

When Christ hung on Calvary's cross, suspended between heaven and earth with blood running down His face, He cried out, " 'It is finished!' " (John 19:30). What was finished? In the Greek text of the New Testament, Jesus' cry "It is finished" is comprehended in the word *tetelastai*. The famous preacher Charles Spurgeon once said, "This one word would need all other words ever spoken to explain it." It has a multifaceted meaning.

Jesus didn't utter this word in defeat. He shouted it in victory.

He didn't utter this word in despair. He proclaimed it in triumph.

He didn't utter this word in desperation. He cried it out in the satisfaction of a completed task. His work on earth was finished. The ransom was complete. He had accomplished His mission. He'd fulfilled the reason God sent Him to earth.

This powerful sentence raises significant questions for our own lives. When we die, will we have finished the work God sent us to earth to do? Or has our object in life been to please ourselves? Have we sought spine-tingling pleasure or heartfelt commitment?

The word *tetelestai* means "to bring to an end," "to complete," "to accomplish the whole scope" of our redemption. Jesus didn't say, "I am finished." He said, "It is finished." His work on earth ended not as a failure but as the completion of a mighty plan. His death on the cross meant that Satan was defeated.

"It is finished"—condemnation, guilt, and shame are gone. Jesus has paid the ransom price. "It is finished"—Satan's power is broken; the chains with which he held us are severed; the prison doors are opened. Jesus has triumphed over the powers of hell. As the hymn writer so majestically states in the old hymn of the church, "Hallelujah! What a Saviour":

Lifted up was He to die,
It is finished was His cry,
Now in heaven exalted high,
Hallelujah! What a Saviour.

Count Ludwig von Zinzendorf, the German prince who started the Moravian mission movement, wrote,

Bold, shall I stand in thy great day,
For who aught to my charge shall lay?
Fully absorbed through these I am,
From sin and fear and guilt and shame.

Never again do we need to fear death. Sin's wage has been paid. In the face of death, the Cross offers hope.

There is a delightful legend that every Romanian schoolchild learns. This legend marvelously reveals the meaning of the Cross.

Once upon a time, there was a Romanian nobleman who lived on a palatial estate. He had extensive land holdings, cattle, horses, sheep, goats, and many servants. A peasant who owned a single cabin and a few sheep and goats lived next to the wealthy man's property.

The wealthy nobleman bribed some townspeople to drive the poor man's animals onto his land at night. Then a trial was held in the town square, and trumped-up charges were brought against the poor peasant. The nobleman claimed that the poor man was irresponsible and should forfeit all of his belongings. So, he lost everything he had. On top of it all, the townspeople mocked him, the nobleman spit on both his cheeks, and the poor peasant had to wander the countryside a penniless beggar.

One day the peasant met the king, who was visiting towns throughout his kingdom. The king listened as the peasant explained his situation. Then the king graciously gave the peasant two large bags of gold—much more than he had lost. And in front of the whole town, the king bent down and kissed the peasant on both cheeks, saying, "Tell everyone that where the evil man spat upon you, the king kissed you. I have now kissed away your shame."

At the Cross, Christ, the King of the universe, gave us much more than we ever lost. At the Cross, He placed the treasure of His own love in our hands. At the Cross, He kissed us on both cheeks. When Jesus shouted, "It is finished," He kissed away our shame. We are children of the kingdom, accepted by the Beloved, kissed on both cheeks by the King of the universe.

"It is finished!" The bondage of guilt, shame, condemnation, fear, sin, and death are broken forever.

In Revelation

The Bible's first book, Genesis, begins with a perfect world, and its last book, Revelation, ends with a perfect world. Revelation shouts "It is finished" for the last time.

Actually, Revelation pictures a twofold "It is finished." The first one comes at the conclusion of the seven last plagues, when a loud voice comes "out of the temple of heaven, from the throne, saying, 'It is done!' " (Revelation 16:17).

The devil has had his day. Darkness, devastation, and death have stalked the land. In the great time of tribulation: Horrible physical sores afflict the bodies of the lost. The seas and rivers turn to blood. The economy collapses. All nature is out of control. A terrible heat wave racks the planet as the sun scorches the unsaved. Darkness covers the earth, bringing freezing temperatures and incredible fear. God withdraws His protective hand, and all hell breaks loose. One unprecedented natural disaster follows another. The plagues follow one another in rapid succession. Earth explodes into its final war—Armageddon is waged as the forces of evil try to destroy the righteous. But God wins, and Satan loses.

What does the expression "It is done" mean in this context?

It means God's appeals for salvation are over. All human beings living on planet Earth have had an opportunity to make their final, irrevocable choice. These choices will determine their eternal destiny. One day, human probation will be over. One day, every person will have had sufficient information to make their decision for or against Christ, and time will no longer matter. If Christ's second coming didn't happen for another hundred or thousand or million years, it wouldn't matter to them. Their choice is fixed. Their decision is made. They have rejected heaven's appeals, and there is no turning back.

Thank God, that day has not yet come. Heaven's gates are open wide. Heaven's appeals are still being given. Heaven's invitation still comes to us today. Our choice today to make Jesus Christ supreme in our lives will settle our eternal destiny. The choices we make today will be fixed in our characters tomorrow.

The Bible reaches its climax with Revelation's second "It is finished" statement. " 'God will wipe away every tear from their eyes; there shall be no more death, nor sorrow, nor crying. There shall be no more pain, for the former things have passed away.' Then He who sat on the throne said, 'Behold I make all things new.' And He said to me, 'Write, for these words are true and faithful.' And He said to me, 'It is done!' " (Revelation 21:4–6).

- Hunger and heartache and horror are over.
- Disease and disaster and death are over.
- Poverty and pain and pollution are over.
- Sickness and sorrow and suffering are over.
- Tears and turmoil and tragedy are over.
- War and weariness and worry are over.
- Confusion and chaos and conflict are over.

Revelation's beast, dragon, and false prophet are cast into the lake of fire; sinners destroyed; and the righteous saved. Christ triumphs. The Holy City descends. A new heaven and a new earth are established. Righteousness reigns, and we are home at last.

Do you want to value yourself as Jesus values you? Do you want to accept His words, the words He spoke on the cross, "It is finished," and let Him free you from the shame, guilt, and bondage of sin? Is it your desire to choose to live for Him today, while the door of mercy is still open? Is it your desire to be home at last, where Jesus reigns eternally?